Earth's Changing Surface

Student Reference Book

ScienceCompanion®
CHICAGO SCIENCE GROUP

WRITERS

Belinda Basca, Rachel Burke, Lance Campbell, and David Sherman

DEVELOPERS

Colleen Bell, Diane Bell, Cindy Buchenroth-Martin, and Catherine Grubin

EDITOR

Wanda Gayle

PEDAGOGY AND CONTENT ADVISORS

Jean Bell, Max Bell, Stephen Harlan*, and Marlyn Payne*

*Scientists or teachers who gave advice but are not part of the Chicago Science Group.

BOOK DESIGN AND PRODUCTION

Happenstance Type-O-Rama; Picas & Points, Plus (Carolyn Loxton)

www.sciencecompanion.com

SBN 10: 1-59192-398-0 ISBN 13: 978-1-59192-398-5

1 2 3 4 5 6 7 8 9 10-BK1, 0411, M8490

www.sciencecompanion.com Chicago Educational Publishing Company, LLC.

Table of Contents

Landscapes, Landforms, and Time

Landscapes and Landforms Surround Us

Land is all around us. The way it looks is different from place to place. In some places, tall mountains tower into the sky. In others, rivers cut through valleys and canyons. Many places are flat, or nearly so, without any mountains, valleys, or hills. Wherever you live or travel, a **landscape** surrounds you.

Word Connection

landscape—A large area of land, or scenery, that can be seen from one place. Landscapes usually have a variety of surface features, such as hills, valleys, and rivers.

Just like a jigsaw puzzle, landscapes are made up of many parts. Tall mountain ranges may be carved with steep canyons. Large areas of prairie may be divided by rivers. A desert may be dusted with sand or scattered with stones.

Since the parts of a landscape can take many forms, these parts are called **landforms.**

Word Connection

landform—A part of the earth's surface that has a unique shape, is easy to recognize, and was created by nature.

Think About It!

Wherever people live, they change the landscape to suit their needs. They build roads, houses, dams, and tunnels. Sometimes they even level hills and fill in wetlands. What is the landscape like where you live? Do you know what the area was like before people lived there? How much do you think it has changed?

Humans change the landscape in many ways.

Landscapes Change over Time

Have you ever heard the saying "as old as the hills"? People say this because nothing else has been around as long as the land—not people, not the things we build, not even the oldest trees.

But the landscape does change. The land around where you live did not always look the way it does today.

Some changes to the landscape happen quickly. Floods, earthquakes, and volcanic eruptions, for example, can change the land in a few minutes. Scientists call events like these **cataclysmic events**.

But most changes to the land happen gradually, over a very long period of time. Some changes take place over hundreds of years, while other changes go on for thousands of years. Some began before the dinosaurs lived on Earth, hundreds of millions of years ago, and they still go on today.

Thinking back to when your parents were your age can seem like ages ago. Looking back 100 years—when there were no computers or TVs, and very few telephones and cars—can seem like ancient times.

Most of the changes to the landscape you will explore started thousands or even millions of years ago, and those changes continue today. Looking back to when most mountains were formed and comparing it to when you, your parents, or even your great-great-grandparents were born is like comparing the size of your room to size of the galaxy. That's a big difference!

Word Connection

cataclysmic event— An event that causes a sudden and dramatic change to the earth's surface.

How Much is a Million?

It would take you about 23 days to count to one million—and that's with no breaks for sleeping, eating, or anything else!

How Much is a Billion?

A billion is a thousand million. It would take you almost 100 years to count to a billion.

2

The Science of Geology

It's Only a Rock. So What?

Let's face it, at first glance, rocks may not seem interesting. They don't talk. They don't eat. They usually just sit there.

But rocks, and pieces of rock, are all around us. They are in the streets we walk on, in the parks where we play, and in the soil where we grow our food.

If you want to learn about the earth around you, rocks are the place to start. And once you look carefully at a rock, you may wonder about other things:

- Where did the rock come from? How was it made?

- Why is the rock shaped the way it is?

- Are there fossils in the rock? What can those fossils tell us?

- Does the rock contain valuable materials, like diamonds or oil, that can be useful to people?

These are the kinds of questions that the scientists who study the earth and its rocks try to answer.

Geologists Study the Planet

For geologists, the people who study the earth, rocks tell a story. A rock may give clues about how a landform got its shape. Or a rock may show scientists that the spot where they are standing looked very different thousands or millions of years ago.

There are many different kinds of geologists. Some geologists try to figure out what materials rocks are made of. Others study the location and movement of water under the earth's surface. Still others might explore volcanoes to learn about how they work and about the rocks that come from them.

Geologists share their knowledge of the earth to help build dams, roads, and buildings. They try to keep us safe by learning about earthquakes and predicting when they might strike. Geologists even travel into space to look down at the Earth to study the continents and different landforms.

Geologists use different tools and work in many places.

💡 Think About It!

In each of these examples, how can geologists' knowledge of the earth help improve people's lives?

- People use products that come from the earth, such as iron, oil, and cut stone.

- Whenever we build a structure—a bridge, a building, or a power plant—we need to know about the ground it will be built on.

- Everything we eat and wear originally came from plants. Plants grow in soil that's partly made up of rock material.

- Geologic hazards, like landslides, volcanic eruptions, earthquakes, and tsunamis, can threaten us and our property.

History of Science and Technology

Sometimes new scientific ideas are born when people use new inventions. You may already know about how the invention of the telescope changed how we see the planets and stars, or that the invention of the microscope helped people see the smallest living things. For the area of science known as geology, the steam engine was just such an invention.

Coal and Canals: Geology 200 Years Ago

Changing Earth Fact

Coal is one kind of natural resource that humans use to heat water and produce electricity. Today, people also use oil and natural gas, which also come from the earth.

In the early 1700s, people only used coal to heat their homes. But by the end of that century, they were burning coal to melt and shape iron, and to power the new steam-driven factories. Coal is a black rock formed from dead plant material that is millions of years old. In some areas, coal lies just below the surface of the earth. In other areas, it's found hundreds of meters beneath the land. As more and more people wanted coal, the people who knew how to locate it became very popular.

During this time, the scientific field of geology became more important to people because they wanted to find the hidden coal, as well as other valuable rocks that lay beneath the earth's surface. But the need for coal created a whole new set of problems that also helped make geology an important new science.

Changing Earth Fact

By 1800, a million tons of coal a year were dug from all of Britain's coal mines.

One of these problems was that coal was bulky. Moving it from mines in the country to the factories and cities where people used it was difficult, especially since few roads at that time were paved.

The OLD-TIME CANAL

In the earliest canals, heavy goods were carried in boats towed by horses.

In the late 1700s, people began to dig canals that filled with water for transportation. Canals allowed people to float heavy loads on boats pulled by horses that walked on a path that ran alongside the canals. Instead of getting stuck on a muddy road, canals enabled goods to be transported in almost any weather, and for a lower price than using carts or wagons. Canal building was all the rage for fifty years, until railroads became cheaper and more dependable.

The need for coal and canals created one of those special moments in history when a clever person makes a remarkable new discovery. In this case, the new discovery came about because of one of the most important skills used by all scientists, even you: the skill of observation.

William Smith: An Early Geologist Makes a Discovery

William Smith, the son of a village blacksmith in England, was the first person to use his observations to make a map of the layers of rock beneath the earth's surface. During the late 1700s, in England, he was hired to help plan two canals that would connect a rich coal mining area with the cities of London and Bristol. All his years of climbing down into mines and watching workers dig canals helped him to notice something no one else had noticed before.

What did he observe that was so important? First, by carefully looking at the underground world, he discovered that the different colored rocks and sediment below the ground were always layered in the same order, like the layers of a cake.

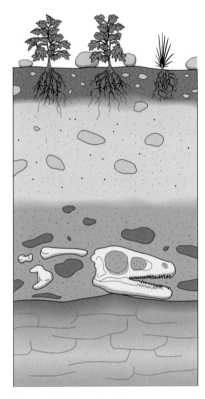

Layers of soil and rock

Word Connection

fossil—A rock whose shape reveals information about an ancient plant, animal, or other organism. If an organism becomes fossilized, that means that its shape or remains have been replaced by rock material.

Second, by looking closely at the rocks in those layers, he discovered that each layer had its own special kind of fossils. One of these fossils was called an ammonite, which is a kind of snail that lived in the ocean millions of years ago.

Different ammonites lived at different times during Earth's long history. When an ammonite became fossilized, it became part of the rock around it. Like a bookmark sticking out from a group of pages, it marked a certain spot in the layers of rock.

By comparing that spot with ammonites from other spots, Smith could tell which layer was which. By looking at the fossils in the earth, anyone could identify the layer of rock and tell when it formed.

Ammonites come many sizes and shapes. This one was found in Montana.

For many years Smith traveled the English countryside collecting sample rocks and fossils. Finally, in 1815, he drew the first map of the types of rocks that make up the surface of England. In fact, this was the very first geological map of its kind anywhere in the world. It helped people understand that the earth was composed of layers. When they asked how he made the map, Smith explained his theory about using fossils to identify the different layers of rock.

Today, geologists still draw maps of the rocks on the surface of the earth and the layers of rock beneath the earth. These maps help scientists and engineers explore the earth, make new discoveries, and form theories about how the earth was formed. But all of today's geologists owe thanks to William Smith for his first map.

People Doing Science

Women in Science

Collecting fossils became a trendy fashion in the mid-1700s. People could not travel safely very far from their homes. But they could travel through time by looking at dusty fossil bones, shells, and plants. Two British women were important fossil collectors during this time.

Ethelred Bennett, who once gave William Smith a piece of fossilized coral to add to his collection, explored and collected fossils all over the county of Wiltshire, England. While most women in her day were learning needlepoint and piano, she was known as an eager fossil hunter by the people who collected them.

Plesiosaur skeleton.

Ichthyosaur.

Another woman, Mary Anning, learned about fossil collecting from her father, who built cabinets for wealthy people to display their fossil collections. In 1811, when she was just 12 years old, she and her brother discovered a complete fossil skeleton of a giant fish. Scientists today know it as an *ichthyosaur*, a kind of dinosaur that swam in the sea millions of years ago. Mary later discovered a fossil of a baby *plesiosaur*, a huge marine reptile, and a nearly perfect fossil of a *pterodactyl*, the winged dinosaur.

Pterodactyl fossil.

Rocks Change and Move

What Is Weathering?

Imagine you're at a park and you reach down to pick up a handful of rocks, pebbles, or sand. Geologists use the term **sediment** to define these pieces of the earth. Where did this sediment come from? Has it always looked like this?

Sediment comes in many sizes, colors, and shapes.

Like landforms, sediment is constantly changing size and shape. And **weathering** is the process responsible for breaking rocks and sediment into smaller pieces.

Weathering can cause rocks like these to crack.

An important type of weathering is known as **abrasion**. Abrasion is the grinding together of one rock against another. It occurs when some force, such as flowing water, causes rocks and sediment to move. As the rocks and sediment move, they grind against other rocks and sediment, and break down into smaller pieces.

Abrasion by rocks and sand can create patterns like the ones in this rock.

A girl plays in a small stream that erodes a sandy beach.

What Is Erosion?

Have you ever sprayed a hose onto the ground and watched what happens to the sediment? As the running water hits the ground, it can loosen sediment and cause it to move with the flowing water. This gradual movement of sediment from one place to another is known as **erosion**.

Sediment may be moved by water, transported by glacial ice, or blown by the wind. For sediment eroded by water and wind, the amount of sediment that will erode depends on the speed of the water or wind. Fast flowing rivers and areas with high wind cause more erosion than slow rivers and areas with little or no wind.

Erosion causes many changes to the landscape. It plays a role in shaping a number of different landforms. For example, moving water is capable of eroding tons of sediment from the sides of a river. Similarly, wind can easily erode sediment on a beach or a sand dune.

Erosion by water can cause ruts in this hillside.

What Is Deposition?

Deposition is related to erosion. After sediment is eroded by moving water, wind, or ice, it will end up somewhere else. The gradual build-up of this eroded sediment is known as **deposition**.

As eroded sediment moves along, some change can cause it to be deposited. For example, moving water or wind may slow down. When this occurs, **gravity** may cause the sediment being carried by the water or wind to settle and deposit on the ground. Or, if the sediment is being eroded by ice, the ice may melt and deposit sediment that was frozen within the ice.

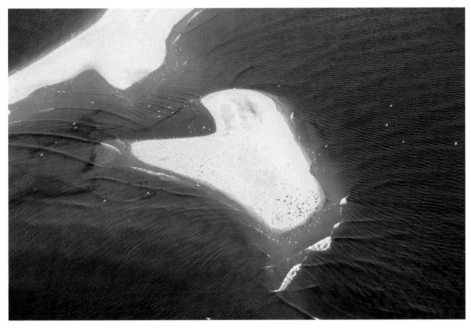

These sand bars were deposited by water.

Like erosion, deposition is usually a very slow process and plays a major role in shaping the surface of the earth. For example, sediment that has been eroded by a river will flow downstream. Eventually, this sediment may be deposited at the shore of an ocean, sea, or lake. If enough sediment is deposited in one area, then a beach may be created.

This sediment will be deposited downstream.

Types of Erosion and Deposition

Some of the ways that moving water, wind, and ice can cause erosion and deposition include the following:

Water

- Rainfall flows down a hillside. Loose sediment erodes and is deposited at the bottom of the hillside.

- Rivers and streams flow down a mountain. They erode sediment from their banks and deposit it downstream.

- Ocean waves and currents erode sand and rocks from beaches and cliffs and deposit sediment along the shore.

Erosion by water can create these small gullies.

Wind

- Wind blows over beaches and sand dunes. Sand erodes from one area and is deposited in another.

- Wind blows over a baseball field. Dirt erodes and is deposited somewhere else.

Wind erodes the sand and deposits it somewhere else.

Ice

- Glaciers slowly creep down mountainsides. As they move, the ice erodes and transports rocks and deposits them down the mountain.

The Path of a River

Thinking About Rivers

Imagine you are standing on the edge of a river. What do you notice? Is the river narrow or wide? Is the water rushing past you or is it gently flowing by? Can you tell where the river begins or where the river ends? Do you know how it got there in the first place?

If you were to return to the edge of the river a year from now, do you think it would look the same? What if you returned ten years from now? Or one hundred years from now? What would the river look like then?

Rivers come in all shapes and sizes. And those shapes and sizes are always changing. Like all landforms, rivers are shaped by the moving water that forms them, and continue to be shaped all the time. Let's take a journey on a river to learn more about where rivers begin, end, and everything in between!

The Parts of a River

Take a moment to review five basic parts of a river:

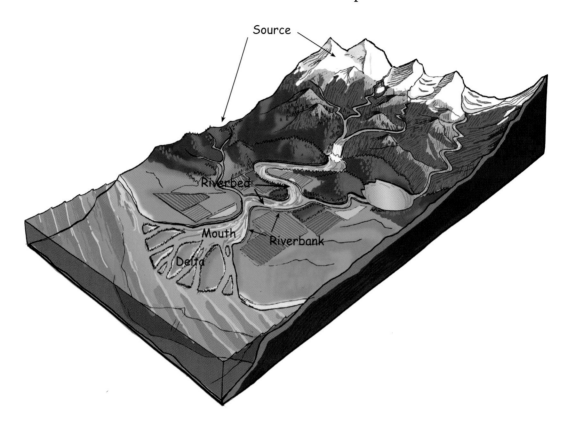

- The **source** is where a river begins. (In the illustration, there are two arrows for the source. That's because a source can be snow on a mountain or a spring that feeds into a river on lower land.)

- The **riverbanks** are the sides of a river.

- The **riverbed** is the bottom of the river. (In the illustration, the riverbed is not visible because the water covers it. The arrow pointing to the river refers to the bottom of the river.)

- The **mouth** is where a river meets a lake, another river, or an ocean.

- The **delta** is a landform at the mouth of a river made by the sand, silt, soil, and rocks deposited by moving water.

How Does Gravity Impact Rivers?

If you drop an apple, the pull of earth's gravity causes it to fall to the ground. Like the apple, water on the earth's surface also falls, or flows, downhill. Eventually, water ends up in a flat place like a lake, sea, or ocean.

A River's Beginnings

The **source**, also called the **headwaters**, is often (but not always) located in the mountains. It may be fed by an underground spring or by runoff from rain, melting snow, or glaciers. As this water flows, it forms small creeks. The force of **gravity** causes these creeks to flow downhill. As they do so, they meet up with other creeks and form streams. These streams continue to combine, becoming larger and larger.

A mountain stream is fast-flowing. As it flows over the earth's surface, it can erode a lot of rocks and sediment. As it erodes, it makes deep valleys with steep sides. Once it begins to cut a valley, the stream gets trapped and carves out the same valley for hundreds, thousands, or even millions of years.

Changing Earth Fact

Some rivers do not begin high in the mountains. An example of this is the second largest river in the United States—the Mississippi River. The Mississippi River's source is only 450 meters (1475 feet) above sea level! That is not very high at all. Its source is a small lake called Lake Itasca in Minnesota. The lake is slightly higher than the surrounding land. Two streams, which get their water from underground springs, send water into Lake Itasca. The water then leaves Lake Itasca, feeding larger lakes and streams, where it eventually forms the Mississippi River!

People Doing Science

Early scientists, explorers, and others searched long and hard for many rivers' sources. Henry Rowe Schoolcraft, a geographer and geologist, is thought to have discovered the source of the Mississippi River. However, he did not do so on his first attempt. In 1821, while on an expedition, he incorrectly identified Cass Lake, a much larger lake east of Lake Itasca, as the source of the Mississippi River.

He later married a Native American woman, Jane Johnson, who descended from the Ojibwa tribe. Schoolcraft learned the Ojibwa language and culture from her. In 1832, during a trip up the Mississippi River to help settle problems between the Ojibwa and Sioux tribes, he discovered the true source of the Mississippi River, Lake Itasca.

Following a River

Changing Earth Fact

The water in very large rivers comes from rain that may have fallen as far away as 6,000 km (4000 mi).

Word Connection

floodplain—A flat area of land stretching out on either side of a river.

As a river continues flowing downhill, the speed of the water and the hardness of the ground affect its shape. As the mountain or hillside becomes less steep, the moving water slows. This causes the river to widen out and the water to slow down (except when it's flooding!). As the moving water slows, it begins to drop, or deposit, the sediment it carried.

Often in these areas, a **floodplain** may develop over time. During heavy rain or snowmelt, this area usually floods. When it floods, sediment carried by the river, including soil rich with nutrients, is deposited in the floodplain. Therefore, floodplain soil is often ideal for growing food.

As a river flows, sediment deposits along its banks. Over time, the river may deposit enough sediment to change its shape.

Depending on the speed of the moving water, the riverbed can erode, and the river may deepen.

As the river reaches level ground, it can become wider. At this point, it may flow quite slowly.

Changing Earth Fact

Floodplains were essential to many ancient civilizations. In ancient Egypt, for example, the Nile River's floodplain was a center of agriculture. The annual flooding of the Nile River renewed the floodplain with water and new soil. It symbolized rebirth for the ancient Egyptians.

A River's End

Eventually all rivers end. This usually occurs when a river reaches a lake, another river, or the ocean itself. The point where a river reaches another body of water is called its **mouth.** Sometimes, a landform called a **delta** may form at the mouth of a river.

Changing Earth Fact

In some arid parts of the world, rivers just disappear into the desert. They do not have enough moving water to make it to the sea. Instead they lose most of their water by evaporation in the dry, hot desert climate and by soaking into the ground.

5

Rivers Shape the Land

The moving water of rivers greatly affects the shape of the land. As they flow, rivers carve out and sculpt the land, creating valleys and canyons. Have you ever seen pictures of the Grand Canyon? It is the result of millions of years of abrasion and erosion by the Colorado River!

Grand Canyon with Colorado River.

Besides making canyons, rivers create floodplains and deltas as they deposit their sediment in new locations. Usually this takes hundreds, thousands, or millions of years. Most of the rivers you see around you formed many, many years ago and have been shaping the landscape ever since.

Changing Earth Fact

The New River, which flows through West Virginia, Virginia, North Carolina, and Tennessee, is considered one of the oldest rivers in the world. While it is impossible to determine its exact age, scientists believe the New River may be as old as 300 million years. The New River is actually what remains of a vast, ancient river called the Teays River, which carved the earth and shaped parts of the eastern United States when dinosaurs roamed the land.

Sometimes, however, heavy rains or rapid snowmelt cause a river to overflow its banks. When an event such as a flood occurs, the earth's surface may change in a short period of time.

How Rivers Get Their Shape

How much, and how quickly, the landscape changes when a river takes another course depends on these factors:

- Slope of the land

- Speed of the water

- Hardness of the earth's surface

- Amount of water

All of these factors should have affected the shape of your rivers. Let's look at each of these factors in more detail.

Slope Affects the Speed of Water

Slope refers to how steep the land is. The greater the slope, the steeper the land is. The slope of the land affects a river's speed. The greater the slope, the faster a river flows.

Steep river.

When a river starts in the mountains, its path is usually very steep, so it flows quickly. Just as you can go faster downhill without pedaling when riding a bike on a steep hill, water can flow faster when it is on a steep slope. As the slope decreases, so does the speed of the water.

Speed of Water Affects a River's Shape

The speed of the water also affects the shape of a river. Often the water may carve deep channels or canyons in the rock. Over many thousands of years, the river can change the shape of the mountains themselves. A V-shaped valley is the result of this type of erosion.

V-shaped valley in Yellowstone National Park, Wyoming.

Faster moving water can carry larger pieces of sediment than slower moving water. As water carries sediment, the sediment bumps and grinds against the riverbed, abrading the rock in the riverbed and carrying it downstream.

As the river reaches level ground, it slows down. It deposits some of its sediment and may no longer flow in a straight path. The river may **meander**, or curve, which further slows the speed of the water, and changes the shape of the landscape.

Meandering river.

By the time a river reaches its mouth, its speed may be very slow. As it enters the relatively still water of another river, a lake, or the ocean, it slows down even more. This causes the river to deposit the rest of its sediment, often creating deltas in the process.

A delta may take several different shapes. One shape is called a "Bird's Foot." This shape forms when the deposited sediment divides the mouth of the river into river **channels**. It takes the shape of a bird's foot. An example is the Mississippi River Delta.

Mississippi River Delta.

Another delta shape is known as a "Fan Shape." This is the most common form of a delta. It usually has the shape of a triangle. An example is the Nile River Delta.

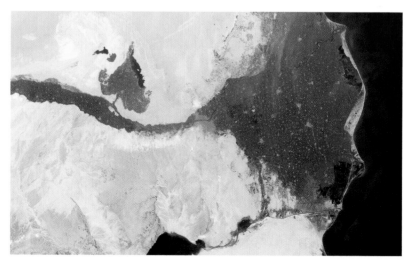

Nile River Delta.

Hardness of the Earth's Surface Affects a River's Shape

The type of rock in the area where a river flows also affects the shape of a river. Soft rocks, such as sandstone, wear down and erode much more easily than hard rocks, such as quartzite. If an area is mostly a soft rock like sandstone, then a river's moving water can wear down and erode the sandstone in the riverbed more quickly than a quartzite riverbed.

Amount of Water Affects a River's Shape

The amount of water in a river affects the type of sediment it can carry. Sand, silt, and clay can be moved over time with just a small stream of water. These small or fine pieces of sediment are easiest to move.

Types of Sediment

The following table shows the sizes of sediment and what they are called.

Sediment	Diameter Size	Size Comparison
Boulder	Greater than 256 mm	Bigger than most adults' feet
Cobble	Between 64 mm and 256 mm	Between a baby's foot and an adult's foot
Pebbles	Between 2 mm and 64 mm	Between the head of a nail and a baby's foot
Sand	Between $1/16$ mm and 2 mm	Between the thickness of your fingernail and the head of a nail.
Silt	Between $1/256$ mm and $1/16$ mm	Between the thickness of a hair and the thickness of your fingernail
Clay	Less than $1/256$ mm	Smaller than the thickness of a human hair

Larger pieces of sediment, such as pebbles, require more water and faster-moving water to move them downstream. And large boulders can only be moved by a large amount of water rushing down a steep slope. Floods can also give rivers the power to move large objects—rocks, cars, and even houses!

Changing Earth Fact

Waterfalls can form when water erodes and carries away large amounts of rock. Niagara Falls in New York and Canada, the second largest waterfall in the world, originally formed seven miles downstream from its current location.

Over time, the water continued to erode the rock away. The rubble of rocks that have broken off the top of the waterfall litters the base of the falls. This process continues to change the landscape. The falls can move up to six feet per year. But don't worry—it's taken 12,000 years for the falls to move seven miles!

Niagara Falls.

Seasonal Floods Shape the Land

When you pour too much water into a cup, the water overflows. The same thing happens to rivers. When there is more water than the river can hold, the water flows over its banks. That overflowing water is called a **flood**.

Water Level of a River

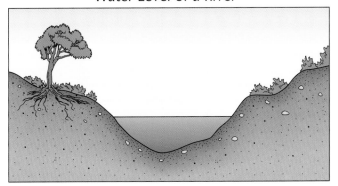

Normal Flow

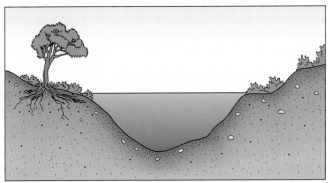

Seasonal Flood

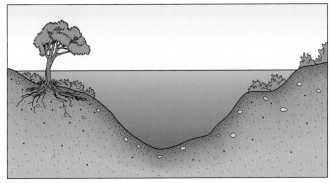

100-Year Flood

Floods are a part of nature. A river or stream near you could be flooding right now. Some rivers flood nearly every year, and most of these floods don't cause much damage.

The extra water can come from an unusually large amount of rain or snow falling in a short amount of time. It can also be the result of rapid snowmelt in the mountains or another area that is at the river's source. It can even be caused by a temporary dam that stops the flow of water and causes it to back up, just like a clogged drain can cause a sink to overflow.

When a river floods, the water spreads into its floodplain. It can remain there for some time, slowly draining, evaporating, and soaking into the soil.

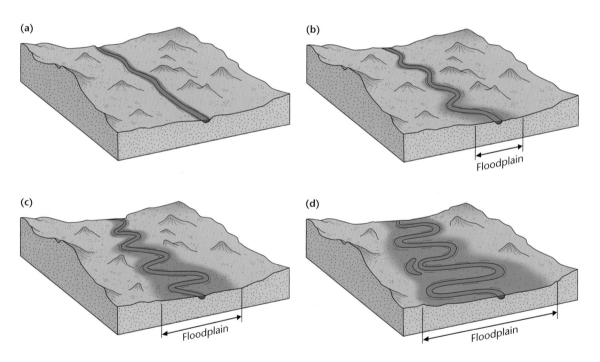

(a)

(b)

Floodplain

(c)

Floodplain

(d)

Floodplain

The **wetlands** that are often part of the floodplains also play a role in a flood situation. Wetlands have a very special quality—they act like a giant sponge, absorbing more water than most land does. During flood times, this helps reduce the amount of water flooding an area.

Eventually, all the floodwaters soak into the earth, evaporate, or return to the original river channel or new channels that have been carved by the flood. It can take hours, days, weeks, or months for the water to return to a normal level.

When rivers flood, they are moving very fast and carry more material than usual downstream. As the river overflows its banks, it widens and slows down. This causes the river to deposit its material in the floodplain. In fact, the soil in floodplains is sediment left behind by floodwaters. Over many years and many floods, the level of the floodplain may actually rise, though the river that flows through it cuts deeper.

> **Word Connection**
>
> **wetland**—An area of land that is covered with water, such as a bog, marsh, or swamp. The water may be there all year, or it may disappear during certain seasons.

Cataclysmic Events

Case Study: Mississippi and Missouri Rivers— The Great Flood of 1993

"It cannot be tamed, curbed or confined...you cannot bar its path with an obstruction which it will not tear down, dance over and laugh at. The Mississippi River will always have its own way, no engineering skill can persuade it to do otherwise..."

—Mark Twain

A large flood can destroy property and endanger people. Each year, floods kill more people than hurricanes, tornadoes, earthquakes, or any other kind of natural disaster.

The Mississippi River **basin**, which includes the Mississippi and Missouri Rivers and all the rivers and streams that flow into them (called tributaries), covers nearly half of the United States. It spreads across 31 states and two Canadian provinces. People living in more than 50 cities rely on water from the Mississippi and Missouri Rivers.

The Great Flood of 1993 was the worst flood in United States history, and one of the country's worst natural disasters ever.

- More than 16,000 square miles of land in nine states were flooded.

- 50 people lost their lives.

- Tens of thousands of people had to leave their homes.

- More than 70,000 homes were washed away or severely damaged.

- More than 1,000 miles of roads and close to half of the bridges across the river were closed.

- 75 towns were completely covered by flood waters.

- In some places, the water remained for almost 200 days.

- Millions of acres of crops were lost; many farmers lost all the money they would have made for the year.[1]

The Great Flood of 1993.

[1]Lee W. Larson. The Great USA Flood of 1993. http://www.nws.noaa.gov/oh/hrl/papers/area/great.htm

Homes and farms threatened by the Great Flood of 1993.

Why Was the Great Flood of 1993 so Bad?

The rainfall in the spring of 1993 was much heavier than usual. But that's not the whole story. To understand why the flood was so bad, you have to look at the land and how people used it.

Today, hundreds of thousands of people live and work in and around the Mississippi River floodplain. They own businesses, live in towns, and go to school in this region because the land is very fertile. The abundant water in the Mississippi River basin also makes it a great place to live and work—except when it floods. And it has always flooded.

When people build houses and streets, some changes can make flooding worse. Water naturally gets absorbed by soil. But water can't seep into concrete—and all those buildings, roads, and park-ing lots create acres and acres of land covered with concrete. Remember how wetlands act like a giant sponge? People can't live on wetlands, so they fill in these low-lying areas with dirt, some-times even building homes there. Every year, acres and acres of wetlands disappear when people move in.

But the story doesn't stop there either. Some of the things people have done to prevent damage from floods can make problems worse when a really big flood occurs. Since the Mississippi River has always flooded periodically—and since people have lived near the river for many years—they have taken many steps to protect lives, land, and property.

The Mississippi River of today looks very different than it did 100 years ago. People have made changes to improve transportation so they could move people, crops, and other products up and down the river.

The modern Mississippi River is shaped much more by humans than it is by anything in nature. Beginning 200 years ago, people living in New Orleans built levees, mounds of dirt that act like walls, to contain the water when floods occur. When a really big flood broke the levees, people rebuilt them, making the new levees taller and stronger to withstand the waters. Many miles of levees were built in the 1930s, after the last truly devastating flood, in 1927. Now there are thousands of miles of levees; they span the length of the river, from Minnesota to Louisiana.

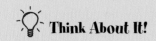

Think About It!

What could be done to avoid having a flood cause so much damage in the future?

If the levees break, they can release a huge amount of water. In 1993, about 5,800 miles (9,300 km) of levees were damaged; many broke and flooded surrounding areas. The St. Louis levee, which is 52 feet (16 m) high, came within two feet of flooding over.

People Doing Science

Flood Prediction

River Flood Warning
National Weather Service, Washington, D.C.
4:15 P.M. EDT Tuesday, June 27, 1995

Heavy rain across the Rappahannock River basin in northern Virginia will cause significant flooding. At 4:10 P.M. the Rappahannock River at Remington was 12.4 feet and rising sharply. The river should reach its 15 foot flood stage tonight and crest between 18 and 20 feet early Wednesday morning.

How can scientists make predictions like this? How do they know in advance how high a river will rise, and when?

To begin with, they collect information about rivers. Scientists measure the depth and amount of water flowing at a particular place. They take these measurements when the river is flowing normally and when the river is flooding. This gives scientists a picture of what happens to a river when it floods.

When possible, scientists who study water, called **hydrologists**, actually take these measurements in person. But they can't be at the same spot everyday. In order to get daily—and even more frequent measurements—scientists use **stream-gaging stations** to collect and send this information.

There are now more than 7,000 stream-gaging stations in the United States that constantly measure and track river flow. More than half of these gaging stations have satellite radios so they send this information to the weather service and other places. Scientists use this information to let people know if they need to evacuate, or leave an area, when there is a big flood.

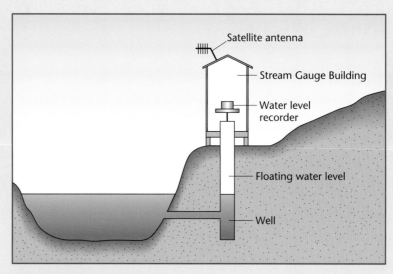

Stream Gauge

They can also collect this information over long periods of time to make predictions about how likely a river is to flood in the future. This makes it possible to create mostly accurate warnings, like the one shown on the previous page.

6

Waves Shape the Shoreline

Anyone who has ever built a sand castle at the beach knows that one wave can knock down hours of effort. The sand can change in just a few hours because of waves. **Waves** contribute to the weathering, erosion, and deposition along the **shoreline**.

Word Connection

waves—The up and down movement of water in a lake or ocean.

Word Connection

shoreline—A boundary line between land and water.

45

How Waves Work

Think About It!

When you were younger, did you ever make waves in the bathtub by pushing down on the surface of the water with a floating toy?

Waves occur when wind blows across the surface of the water. This causes the water to move up and down, resulting in waves. Because wind's energy causes the water to move, this type of energy is sometimes called **wave energy**.

Along an ocean or lake's rocky cliffs and shorelines, the constant force of water crashing against the shore wears away softer rock, leaving behind rock that resists erosion. Waves also hurl pebbles and sand against rock, another example of abrasion caused by water.

Eventually, wave action carries away the sediment that is created, which may later wash up on shore and form a sandy beach. This type of weathering can create an endless variety of arches, caves, cliffs, and sea stacks.

Over time, waves weather and erode sea arches.

Waves Form the Beach

Beaches form in shallow waters where waves break and wash ashore. The waves carry sediment onto the land. As the **backwash** soaks into the beach or drains away, the sediment is left behind.

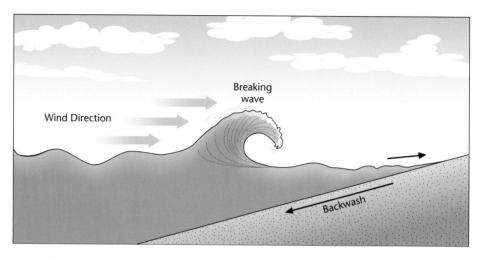

A breaking wave along a shoreline.

Waves erode a beach or deposit new sediment depending on their strength. Tall and frequent **destructive waves** erode beaches; small and slow **constructive waves** build beaches.

There are also seasonal changes to beaches. Winter storms produce more frequent destructive waves. These waves can destroy or significantly shrink beaches by eroding away the sand. But when winter storms depart, the calmer constructive waves of summer steadily rebuild the beach. (Of course, even a severe summer storm, like a hurricane, can cause severe beach erosion!)

Waves and Wind Help and Hurt Coasts

Along the seashore in some parts of the world, wind and water work together to deposit sand and create low-lying islands called **barrier islands**. Depending on the strength of the wind and waves, these islands constantly build up, shift, or wear down.

These islands have sandy beaches that make them popular with people who like to swim, surf, and play near the water's edge. They are a popular vacation destination, attracting tourists to the coasts of Texas, Louisiana, and Florida, the Sea Islands of Georgia, and the Outer Banks of North Carolina.

Topsail Beach, North Carolina. Before and after Hurricane Fran, which struck in 1996.

The same water and wind that make barrier islands so attractive, can also threaten them. As you know, hurricanes can cause sudden, severe erosion by creating huge waves that carry away beaches and the houses, hotels, and towns built on them.

Word Connection

breakwaters and seawalls—Structures built by humans to prevent erosion of a shoreline.

Human activities can increase erosion. People often try to protect houses and hotels from storms by building **breakwaters** and **seawalls**. These structures can protect buildings from —erosion, but they also block new sand from being deposited on the beach. Over time, more sand is removed by erosion than is deposited by waves. Waves can then wear away more and more sand. Eventually, the seawalls weaken and collapse, leaving the buildings vulnerable to waves. If a strong storm comes along, the damage can be tremendous.

Coastal erosion costs hundreds of millions of dollars a year. Some of these costs are from the damage caused by storms and flooding. Other costs come from the need to prevent erosion. In some places, new sand must be trucked in and spread onto beaches. Also, many experts predict that continued global warming will cause sea levels to rise, resulting in more coastal erosion.

Breakwater along the San Diego coastline.

Seawalls prevent erosion by crashing waves.

River Connection–Building Dams

There are many dams on rivers in some regions of the United States, including the states near the western Gulf of Mexico, the west coast, and parts of New England. Dams on rivers make the problem of erosion on river beaches even worse. People build dams for many good reasons. They prevent floods that can kill people and damage property. Many of us drink water that was stored by a dam or eat food that was grown with water from behind a dam. **Reservoirs**, the human-made lakes behind dams, also provide people with places for recreation.

Sediment can build up behind dams like this one in Washington State.

But dams prevent rivers from flowing freely to the ocean. Since the dammed rivers can't flood or flow fast, any sediment they carry is trapped in the water behind the dam instead of eventually floating out to sea or forming a delta or beach. Without new sediment, delta sediment and beach sand cannot be replaced.

A Brief Guide to Rocks

Knowing About Rocks

There are a lot of different rocks to learn about. But how many have you actually seen or touched?

You've probably heard of people locating precious metals like gold, silver, and copper deep in "mother lodes" in Earth's rock layers. You may have heard of gems like diamonds, rubies, or emeralds being found inside the earth. You've probably even played with rocks of all types in your yard, neighborhood playground, or near a river, stream, or mountain.

Copper can be processed and shaped into a plumbing fixture.

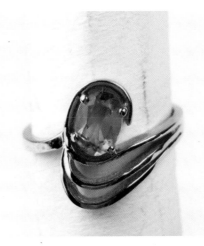

This emerald has been cut and set in a gold ring.

But, it would take hundreds of pages to write about all the types of rocks on Earth. Instead, this short guide will help you become familiar with the ones you might use in science class.

Learning More About Rocks

Since your class may investigate the types of rocks called limestone, pumice, quartzite, sandstone, and slate, review the following sections to learn more about them.

Limestone

Word Connection

sedimentary rock—Rock that forms when sediment or the remains of plants and animals are cemented together.

Limestone is a **sedimentary rock** that is often formed from the shells, skeletons, and other remains of ancient sea life. Water that is acidic (containing acid substances) can dissolve limestone. This is why caves and caverns form in areas where there is a lot of limestone.

Limestone is often whitish gray and feels chalky.

Pumice

Pumice is an **igneous rock** that forms during explosive volcanic activity. It is usually found near active or extinct volcanoes. Pumice is the only rock on Earth that will float in water.

Pumice is very light and breaks down easily.

Word Connection

igneous rock—Rock that forms when molten rock cools and hardens.

Quartzite

Quartzite is a **metamorphic rock** that is formed when sandstone gets tremendous heat and pressure. The heat and pressure causes the rock to become harder, which makes it more resistant to erosion. Much of the sand found on ocean beaches comes from weathered quartzite.

Quartzite is very hard to break down.

Word Connection

metamorphic rock—Rock that forms when other rocks change because of chemical reactions, heat, pressure, or all three.

Sandstone

Sandstone is a very common sedimentary rock that is formed when sand grains are cemented together. Depending on the material that cements the grains, the rock may be white, gray, or red. The sandstone you'll be working with is red because the cementing material has iron in it.

Sandstone feels like fine sandpaper.

Slate

Slate is a metamorphic rock that is formed when a type of rock called shale gets under intense heat and pressure. Shale is made up mostly of compressed particles of clay and is usually a very soft rock. When shale metamorphoses and becomes slate, the rock that results is much harder and more brittle.

Slate looks like thin sheets of rock stacked on top of each other.

Glaciers—How Ice Shapes the Surface of the Earth

Ice is a mighty sculptor of the landscape. It can carve wide valleys and deposit large amounts of sediment. In high mountains, and in the polar regions, ice plays a major role in shaping the landscape.

Just how does something solid, like ice, shape the earth?

What Is a Glacier?

Think About It!

There are 204 glaciers in Canada and the United States. Where in these two countries do you think most of these glaciers are located?

Word Connection

evaporate—The process of a liquid changing into an invisible gas.

A **glacier** is a huge mass of moving ice that is so big and thick it does not change much during the seasons. Glaciers form over many years—and they only form under the following conditions:

- Lots of snow needs to fall.

- The climate has to be cool enough year-round. Even though some of the snow melts or **evaporates** during the summer, some snow stays all year.

- The layers of snow build up over hundreds and thousands of years.

- When enough glacial ice forms, the glacier flows downhill under the force of gravity.

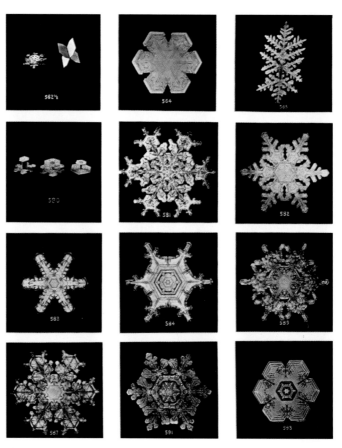

These are some of the first photographs ever made of snowflakes. They were taken over a hundred years ago by an amateur photographer named Wilson Bentley.

Snow Turns into Ice

There's more to a glacier than deep snow. Snowflakes are **crystals** made of frozen water. Between the frozen water there are air spaces. In fact, there can be more air in the spaces of a snowflake than there is water! That's why newly fallen snow is often light and fluffy.

Now think about what happens when you make a snowball. As you pack the snow together with your hands, the ball of snow becomes icier and harder—and, even though it may be smaller than it was to begin with, it becomes heavier as you add more snow. This happens because, as you pack the snow, you crush the crystals together, pushing out the air. The heat from your hands also melts some of the crystals. This melted water becomes ice when it gets cold and freezes again.

The same things happen as more snow piles up on a glacier. The layers of snow are **compressed** until almost all of the air is squeezed out. At the deepest layers, the snow crystals turn to ice.

Changing Earth Fact

Without air in it, the ice in the lower layers of a glacier looks blue instead of white. The snow and ice higher up still has air so it looks white.

Changing Earth Fact

When all the air is squeezed out of ice in a glacier, it becomes very hard; it takes a lot of heat to make this ice melt. In fact, scientists describe this kind of ice, in the deepest layers of glaciers, as a type of rock.

From Snow to Ice

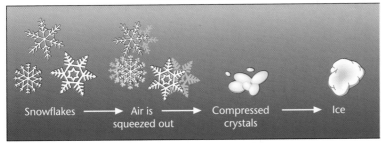

Snowflakes ⟶ Air is squeezed out ⟶ Compressed crystals ⟶ Ice

Glaciers Move!

A glacier isn't just a huge mass of ice and snow that never melts. Remember, in order to be considered a glacier, this ice must also move.

Think About It!

What does the glacier in this picture remind you of?

Some people think glaciers look like huge rivers of ice. Of course, if you visit a glacier, you won't see it flow, the way you could see a river flow. That's because glaciers usually move incredibly slowly—as slow as 2.5 to 5 centimeters (1–2 inches) a day.

Why do glaciers move? The answer is gravity and weight.

If the glacier is on a slope, especially a steep slope, the ice will move downhill over time. Even though ice is frozen water, there is so much weight in a glacier, that it moves very, very slowly, like candle wax that's just slightly warmed.

Another reason why the glacier moves is that some of the ice at the bottom melts. Wet ice is very slippery. The ice of the glacier slowly slides down this slick surface.

Glaciers generally move downhill, or **advance**. They may lose some snow and ice each year, during the warmer months, as a result of melting and evaporation. But, as long as more snow is added during the colder months than is lost in the warmer months, a glacier will continue to grow and advance.

The Retreat of a Glacier

A partially melted glacier reveals changes to the landscape.

If more snow is lost than is replaced each year, a glacier will begin to shrink. Though it may still flow and move downhill, if more ice melts from the lower part of a glacier than is replaced from above, the glacier appears to **retreat**.

When a glacier retreats and melts away completely, you can really see how the landscape has changed.

Glaciers Shape the Earth's Surface

Like giant earth-moving machines, glaciers scrape the earth beneath them, breaking off rock as they move. Like rivers, glaciers carry rock material along as they move, eventually depositing it somewhere else. When glaciers weather, erode, and deposit rock, they shape the earth's surface in unusual and interesting ways.

A view from space of mountains shaped by glaciers.

Glaciers Weather Rock

Glaciers weather rock in a number of ways. They pluck rock as they move down steep mountainsides. Over time, the bits of rock and sediment freeze into the ice, giving the underside of a glacier a gritty texture. As they move into flatter areas, the ice and rocks continue to abrade the earth's surface.

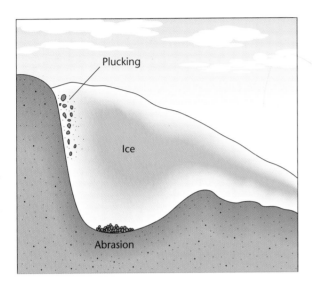

Like sandpaper on wood, the glacier polishes the rock it slides over. After the ice melts, the exposed rock can have a smooth, shiny look. Geologists describe rock with this appearance as having **glacial polish**.

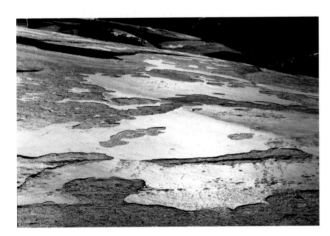

Glacial polish and glacial striations show the effects that glaciers have on rocks.

Glaciers can also cut long scratches in the rock, called **glacial striations**. These striations help geologists figure out the direction that the glacier moved when it flowed.

Glaciers Erode Rock

Glaciers move more slowly than rivers, but over time their huge size and weight can make them more powerful. Compared to rivers, glaciers can carry sediment of almost any size—from very small pebbles and bits of soil to huge boulders the size of cars and houses. The ice pushes this unsorted mixture of debris into mounds or ridges, called **moraines**, along its sides and front.

Some moraines are only a meter high, others can be hundreds of meters tall. Lakes often form behind moraines after a glacier melts.

Sometimes a piece of ice can break off of a glacier and get buried in a moraine. When the ice eventually melts, it can leave a small scooped-out area, called a **kettle**. When kettles fill with water they can create small kettle ponds or larger kettle lakes.

Alpine (mountain) glaciers can erode a steep mountainside and create a rounded hollow, or depression, shaped like a shallow bowl. This kind of feature is called a **cirque**. After the glacier melts, the cirque can fill with water to form an **alpine lake**.

Mountain glaciers carve interesting features into the landscape.

Horns, such as Kinnerly Peak in Glacier National Park, Montana (shown on this page), are created when several cirque glaciers erode the sides of a mountain. The rock is scraped away from the peak until all that is left is a steep, pointed peak with sharp ridges leading up to the top.

Glaciers Deposit Rock

What starts out as a jumbled mess of rocks and other material of all different sizes sorts out and gets deposited in different ways over time.

Moraines (described on page 64) are one landform created when a glacier erodes rock. In some areas where glaciers existed long ago, you can still see the moraines that were deposited by large glaciers. Cape Cod, in Massachusetts, is an example of a huge moraine left behind by a giant glacier that melted.

Cape Cod, Massachusetts was formed by a huge glacier.

Erratics can look like giant boulders that have been left stranded.

Some glaciers can carry truck-sized boulders hundreds of miles. When the glacier retreats, the melting ice deposits the boulders. Often, no other large rocks are found nearby. These large rocks are called **erratics** because they can be rocks that don't match the rocks found in the local area.

The following picture shows how glaciers can create many of these landforms to create complex landscapes.

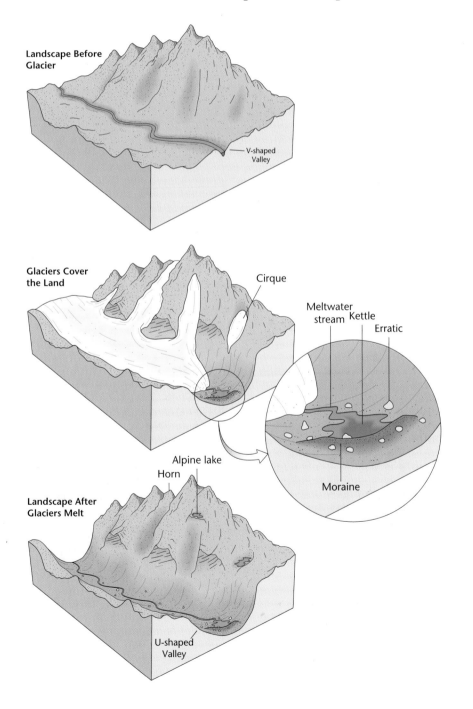

Landscape Before Glacier

V-shaped Valley

Glaciers Cover the Land

Cirque

Meltwater stream   Kettle

Erratic

Moraine

Alpine lake

Horn

Landscape After Glaciers Melt

U-shaped Valley

Why Are Glacial Valleys Shaped Differently Than River Valleys?

Think About It!

Look at the images above. Why do glaciers carve the land differently than rivers?

Try It Out!

Glaciers are made of ice and rivers are made of water. Think of a solid, then a liquid. Pour some water over a rock, and then rub a piece of ice over the rock with some pressure. What differences do you think there will be between the two processes? How could this affect the valley formations shown above?

A river makes a V-shaped valley because the water continues to dig its path deeper and deeper into the earth and rock underneath it. The walls have a more-or-less uniform slope from top to bottom; the slopes erode over time.

Most glaciers start to form where a V-shaped river valley already exists. Glaciers erode on all sides, and scrape away everything in their path, so the walls remain steep and the valley becomes broad and U-shaped. When you think about how much rock and soil is carved away to turn a V-shaped valley into a U-shaped valley, it is easy to see why glaciers can create large moraines at the end of a glacial valley.

The Biggest Glaciers of All

The photographs of glaciers you've seen so far are all mountain or valley glaciers. But there's another kind of glacier that's even larger. These glaciers—giant sheets of ice called **continental glaciers**—can only be found in two places on the earth, in Greenland and Antarctica.

A view from space of the ice-covered island of Greenland.

A computer-generated view from space of the "frozen continent," Antarctica.

It's hard to imagine just how huge these glaciers are. Although there are more than 150,000 mountain glaciers around the world, these two massive sheets of ice contain more than 90% of all the glacial ice on earth. In fact, there is enough ice in Antarctica to cover the whole United States with a sheet of ice 3 kilometers (nearly 2 miles) thick. In some places, the ice on these glaciers is more than 4½ kilometers (nearly 3 miles) thick!

At one time much of the land in the northern hemisphere, including large parts of North America, was covered with glacial ice, just as Antarctica is now. You'll learn more about how the earth looked then, and how it shaped the landscapes we see today, in the next chapter, when you read about the Ice Ages.

9

The Ice Ages

What Is an Ice Age?

An ice age is a period of hundreds to thousands of years when the **climate** on the earth becomes colder and wetter and much of the earth's northern hemisphere is covered by glacial ice. There have been several ice ages in the earth's history. The most recent ice age is often referred to with capital letters as the **Ice Age**. It began about two million years ago and ended about 12,000 years ago.

Glaciers, especially huge continental glaciers like the sheet of ice covering Antarctica, take tens of thousands of years to build up. In fact, most of today's glaciers—which cover about 10 percent of the earth's surface—are left over from the last ice age.

Word Connection

climate—The average weather for a particular place over time. Instead of describing how hot or cold it is on a particular day, and whether it's snowing or raining, it describes what the weather usually is for the place at different times of the year.

During the Ice Age, one-third of the earth's land area was covered by glaciers. Almost all of Canada, as well as much of the northern United States, was covered with ice.

Most of the glaciers that exist today are the remains of glaciers that were formed during the last Ice Age. The light gray areas on the map below show how much land, in North America and the Arctic, the glaciers covered 20,000 years ago.

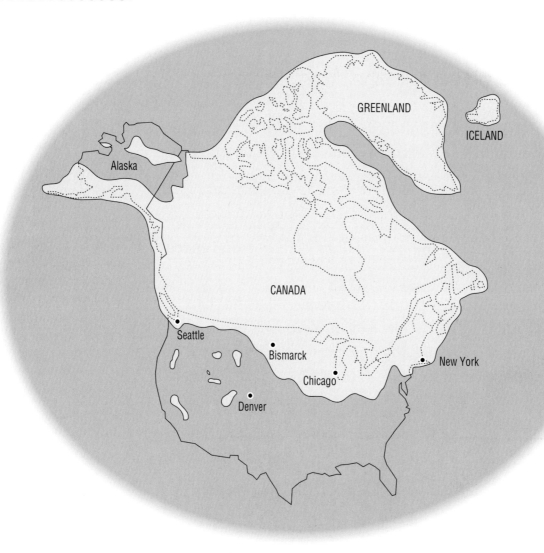

How Cold Is It During an Ice Age?

Today, the average temperature around the world is 14°C (58°F). In some places, like Antarctica, it is much colder, and in other places, like Africa, it is much hotter.

During the Ice Age, the average temperature was around 10°C (50°F)—just four degrees Celsius less than the average temperature today. This may not seem like a lot, but back then it was enough to put many parts of the world into a deep freeze, one cold enough and long enough, to create the vast glaciers of the Ice Age.

How Did the Last Ice Age Shape North America's Landscape?

The huge glaciers of the Ice Age did much more than sculpt U-shaped valleys, scrape the rock, and dump moraines and other deposits on the land. Much of the rich soil of the Midwestern United States was deposited by glaciers, and the way the Ohio River drains was influenced by these glaciers. The Great Lakes in the northern United States were also scooped out by these glaciers.

Changing Earth Fact

Long Island, in New York, is a moraine that was deposited during the last Ice Age, around 15,000 years ago.

The Great Lakes from space.

Areas in the northeastern United States or the northern Midwest states with these features were probably shaped by the giant ice sheets:

- Stony soil

- Hills dotted with lakes

- Scratched and grooved rock surfaces

- Long, low ridges made of sand and pebbles

Why Do Ice Ages Begin and End?

No one knows for sure why ice ages start and why they end, but scientists have several ideas.

- In very ancient times, the depth of the oceans may have played a role. If the ocean is shallow, the sun warms the water more; if it is deeper, the water is colder.

- Scientists think that more recent ice ages might have been affected by how much Earth tilts, or wobbles, on its axis. When part of Earth is tilted away from the sun, the climate there is colder.

- Once these giant ice sheets start to form, they help keep an ice age going because they reflect the sun's energy away from the earth and prevent the land from warming up.

When the climate around the world gets warmer, ice ages end and glaciers begin to melt. Many of the causes for this are natural, but there is one cause that has developed in the past 100 years or so. You may have heard the term **global warming**. Many scientists think that global warming, caused by humans, is speeding up how quickly the world's glaciers are melting.

Global Warming

What Is Global Warming?

Have you ever gotten into a car that's been sitting closed up in the sun on a hot summer day? Or been in a greenhouse in early spring, when it's still too cool for plants to grow outside? The greenhouse may be as warm as a tropical island, while you still need to wear a coat outside. The car and the greenhouse both trap air, heated by the sun, inside.

In the same way, gases in the earth's **atmosphere** trap heat energy from the sun's rays. Scientists call this the **greenhouse effect**. If none of the sun's energy was trapped, Earth would be a very cold place, so cold that it would not be possible for humans or lots of other animals and plants to survive.

Earth's climate has always changed. What concerns scientists is how quickly those changes have taken place in recent years. In the last 100 years, the earth's surface has warmed about .5°C (1°F). This may not seem like much, but remember that the difference between the comfortable climate we have today and the last Ice Age was just 5°C (9°F). In fact, the year 1990 used to be the warmest ever recorded, but that record has been broken almost every year since then. In fact, scientists believe the world is warmer now than at any time in the past 1000 years.

Some of the reasons for the warming climate may be natural. At different times in the earth's history, the climate has been warmer or colder. But scientists also think that some things that people do are causing this rise in the temperature.

Word Connection

atmosphere—
The thin layer of gases—mostly nitrogen (78%), oxygen (21%), other gases and water vapor (1%)—surrounding Earth. The air all around us.

What Causes Global Warming?

In the past, humans lived much more simply. There were no cars, no trains, no planes. People did not have electricity or any other energy source, besides fire, to heat their homes, cook food, or make any of the other tasks of everyday life easier.

Beginning about 200 years ago, people began to use machines to help them do a lot of their work. This period is called the **Industrial Revolution**. It changed the way that many people live, in large and small ways, making our lives much easier. But these changes may also be the reason that Earth's climate is getting warmer.

Over the past 100 years, people have used more and more machines, and more and more energy to run these machines. Much of the energy used to run our machines comes from electricity. Every day we use electricity to light and heat our houses, to cook food, to wash clothes and heat the water to wash ourselves, to watch TV, and to run computers and other equipment.

Electricity comes from power plants. Most power plants use coal and oil to make electricity. Burning coal and oil produces carbon dioxide, one of the gases called a **greenhouse gas**. Whenever we drive or ride in a car, we are also adding greenhouse gases to the atmosphere.

Word Connection

greenhouse gases— A group of gases— including water vapor, carbon dioxide, methane, ozone, and other gases—that trap the sun's heat energy in Earth's atmosphere, producing a greenhouse effect.

Other things we do send greenhouse gases into the air, too. Some of the trash that we send to landfills produces a greenhouse gas called methane. Methane is also produced by the cows, pigs, and chickens we raise for food. And, when factories make the things that we buy and use every day, they too can send greenhouse gases into the air.

How Does Global Warming Change the Earth's Surface?

Many scientists believe that today's temperature increase of one degree is already changing the landscape. They have observed that glaciers around the world are melting and that glacial ice is not as thick as recorded earlier. Temperatures in Antarctica are actually rising twice as fast as other places in the world, causing the ice to melt. The largest block of ice in Antarctica, the Ward Hunt Ice Shelf, which had been around for 3,000 years, began cracking in 2000, split apart in 2002, and is now breaking into pieces and drifting out to sea, where it will melt.

When glaciers melt, most of the water eventually flows to the ocean. The continental glaciers in the polar regions store a lot of water, about 2% of Earth's water. If these huge glaciers melt, that water would be added to the oceans, causing the sea level to rise. Indeed, over the last 100 years, the level of the sea has risen about 6–8 inches worldwide. Scientists know this is so because they have taken measurements and have seen that the high tides today are higher than they were in the past. (When the sea level rises, the tide goes farther up the beach.)

What Might Happen If Global Warming Continues?

Scientists are not fortune-tellers. They don't know exactly what will happen in the future. But they can use special computer programs to predict how the climate may change in the years ahead. And the computer programs, along with the melting glaciers and rising seas, provide some good clues. They tell us that the Earth's

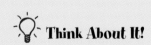 **Think About It!**

The average elevation of the state of Florida is about 30 m (100 feet). What do you think would happen to places like Florida if the polar ice caps completely melted and the sea level rose 30–50 feet?

temperature will probably continue to rise as long as we continue releasing so many greenhouse gases into the atmosphere.

Sea level may rise between several centimeters and as much as one meter during the next century. This will affect both natural systems and man-made structures along coastlines. Coastal flooding could cause saltwater to flow into areas where salt is harmful, threatening plants and animals in those areas.

> ## Changing Earth Fact
>
> If all glacial ice melted, sea level would rise approximately 70 meters worldwide.

Places like this could be eroded or flooded by rising sea levels.

Oceanfront houses and other buildings, especially in areas close to sea level like Florida, could be affected by flooding. Beach erosion could make this problem even worse. Moving these houses or building barricades to protect them from the rising sea could cost billions of dollars. Flooding could also reduce the quality of drinking water in coastal areas.

Global warming may make it possible to grow crops in areas that are currently too cold. But it might make it impossible for crops to grow in other areas. For example, in Kansas, where a type of wheat called "winter wheat" is grown, warmer winter temperatures could prevent the freezing temperatures that kind of wheat needs as part of its growth cycle. A rise in summer temperatures could also create **droughts**, drying out cropland. In some parts of the world, people may not have enough to eat because they will not be able to grow the food they need.

Word Connection

drought—A long period without significant rainfall.

How Can People Help Slow Global Warming?

If people make changes in how they live and begin to **conserve**, or use less, energy whenever possible, it may be possible to slow down global warming. Here are some ways that people conserve energy today:

- Drive a car that gets better mileage. A car that get 30 miles per gallon burns half the fuel, and produces half the greenhouse gases, than a car that gets 15 miles per gallon. A hybrid car that combines a gas engine with an electric motor, can get as much as 50 miles per gallon and reduce greenhouse gases even more.

- Ride the bus, subway, or train. Ride a bicycle or walk to reduce the use of fossil fuels to zero!

- Use more energy-efficient light bulbs. About twenty-five percent of all the electricity produced in North America is used
  just to make light. A **compact fluorescent bulb** (or **CFL**),
  uses less than half the electricity than an **incandescent
  bulb** does to produce the same amount of light.

Changes like these can help reduce greenhouse gases and protect
Earth from global warming.

Shaping Rock

The Role of Water

Many people think that desert land-forms, like this one, are shaped by the wind. But they are only partly correct.

Even though water is often absent from a desert, it is responsible for shaping much of the landscape. Water can weather and erode solid rock to create a number of fascinating landforms, such as **hoodoos**. A hoodoo is a term for rock formations like **mushroom rocks** and **rock pillars**.

Water can act in different ways to shape hoodoos. For example, rainfall can weather and erode these formations as it streams down the sides. Also, water can enter cracks in the rock. If the water repeatedly freezes and thaws, the rocks can break down and fall apart due to these forces.

This rock pillar was mostly weathered by moving water and ice.

This mushroom rock was mostly weathered by moving water and ice.

Hoodoos are often oddly shaped rocks that are left in place because a hard **cap rock** protects a column of softer rock below it. The cap rock prevents rainfall from weathering and eroding the softer rock below.

Changing Earth Fact

A myth of the Paiute Indians says that some hoodoos are ancient "Legend People." They were turned into stone as a punishment for bad deeds.

Hoodoos attract photographers from around the world because their shapes are often so unusual and sometimes even eerie.

The hard caps on these mushroom rocks protect the rock below.

The Role of Wind

Compared to water and ice, wind does not have much of an effect on the shape of hoodoos. However, wind does play a part in smoothing the surfaces of these landforms.

Wind has the most effect in areas where there is a lot of sand combined with strong and steady winds. Wind picks up the sand which then abrades the rock surfaces. Given enough time, wind-blown sand can smooth rock surfaces like sandpaper can smooth most kinds of rough material.

11

Blowing in the Wind

The Making of Sand

Most sand that ends up in dunes begins as part of a mountain. As the rock the mountain is made of weathers, sediment washes downhill into rivers or streams. The sediment breaks into smaller and smaller pieces as it bounces and rolls in the flowing water.

Some sediment eventually becomes small enough to be called sand. The moving water of rivers and streams polishes the sand. Some sand flows all the way to the ocean, some ends up on shores of lakes, and some is deposited in desert regions.

Then wind helps them attain their final shape. As the wind blows sand grains into obstacles and each other, they become shaped like tiny balls.

Changing Earth Fact

It can take millions of years for a sand grain to form and travel to the ocean.

Types of Sand

There are a number of different types of sand. The shape, color, and size of the sand grains depend on the rocks the sand came from.

- The black sand beaches of Hawaii are made of particles of volcanic rock.

- The white dunes of White Sands, New Mexico are made of the mineral **gypsum.**

- Many dunes throughout the world are made of the golden-colored mineral quartz.

Beaches with volcanic rock and sand can be found in many places on the Hawaiian Islands.

This close up of white sand dunes makes them look as soft as pillows.

Although most sand comes from weathered rocks and minerals, sand can also be made of the skeletons of animals. For example, some beaches in the Caribbean and other areas are made from shells and coral that have been crushed by ocean waves.

It takes a lot of crushed coral to make a beach.

Wind and Sand

If you've ever been to a sandy beach or a dusty field during a wind storm, you've probably experienced how the wind can erode bits of sediment.

A gentle breeze of 16 km/hr (10 mph), about as fast as you can run, can erode fine sand grains. Wind speeds of about 32 km/hr (20 mph), or about as fast as an average dog can run, can erode most sand grains.

The smallest grains might be carried for long distances by the wind, while the larger grains tend to lift a few feet off the ground, fall back to Earth, and then bounce along before being lifted again.

Sand Dunes

Like water and ice, wind plays an important role in shaping the earth. One interesting and beautiful way that wind sculpts the earth is by creating sand dunes. Sand dunes form throughout the world in deserts, near ocean beaches, on lake shores, and along rivers. In fact, dunes may form anytime there are the following conditions:

- Dry and loose sand

- A strong and steady wind

- An area large enough for sand to blow around

There's plenty of sand, wind, and space for these dunes to form.

You may think of deserts as being covered with sand. In fact, less than one-fifth of Earth's total desert area is covered with sand. And sand dunes only make up a tiny fraction of deserts in North America.

These dunes are located in California in the Mohave Desert.

The Making of a Dune

Some dunes form when the wind meets an obstacle, like a rock or a plant. This deposits the sand in front of the obstacle, like a soccer ball is blocked by a goalie. Eventually, a small mound of sand piles up in front of the obstacle. As the sand piles up, it blocks more wind, depositing more sand.

If the wind continues to blow, the sand will move to the top of the pile until the pile is so steep that it collapses and flows down the other side of the pile.

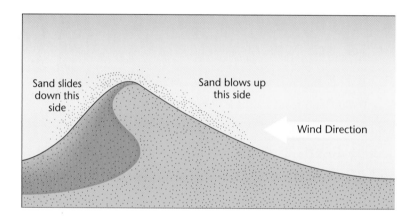

Dunes Can Walk

A dune can grow and begin to move, or "walk" in the same direction as the wind. Sand erodes from one side of the dune and rolls and bounces up to its top. When it reaches the top of the dune, it tumbles down the other side and forms a steep slope. When the slope gets too steep, a layer of sand breaks free and slides down the face. When this process happens over and over, the growing dune inches forward.

Dunes "Boom" and "Bark"

People throughout the world have noticed strange sounds coming from sand dunes. In some areas, a noise similar to thunder results when sand slides down the face of a dune. Other sliding dunes tend to make noises like barking dogs or sea lions. What causes some dunes to produce these unusual sounds? Geologists are not sure, but they think the sand must be very dry, very rounded, and finely polished compared with normal, silent sand for barking or booming to occur.

> **Changing Earth Fact**
>
> Astronomers think that the phenomena of booming dunes may even be common in the extremely dry sand dunes on Mars!

Booming dunes are located all over the world. You can find them in Africa, the Middle East, South America, and North America.

Plants and Dunes

Dunes provide habitats for plants that are adapted to the weather and soil conditions of their regions. Grasses that grow in the dunes along a number of coastal regions get nutrients from tiny organisms and minerals that the ocean breezes bring in. Also, seaweed and organic debris along the beach are blown inland, decompose, and provide nutrients for the plants.

The grasses growing in these dunes help to hold the sand in place.

Often the first plants able to grow on any dune can thrive in the sandy soil. As these plants take hold, they send down deep roots to use the small amounts of available water. When these plants die, the breakdown of this plant material helps change the sand into a more plant-friendly soil.

Humans and Dunes

Humans have not always been successful as we try to adapt to the changing conditions of dunes. As human civilization encroaches on sand dunes, we often try various methods to prevent the dunes from "walking all over us." In some cases, dunes have expanded and swallowed entire coastal towns.

In the early 1900s, the dunes along the Oregon coast began to drift onto roads or bury homes. Early settlers who destroyed the natural dune vegetation were partly to blame for this sand movement. So in the 1930s, people planted European beach grass, along with other plants, in an effort to control the dune movement. Plants can help to keep dunes from moving because their root systems can prevent sand erosion.

Unfortunately, the beach grass grows faster than any of the **native plants** and has greatly affected the natural cycles of life in the dune area.

Cataclysmic Events: Wind

Hurricanes

The most catastrophic type of storm on Earth, hurricanes are "tropical storms" that form over the ocean. Storms become classified as hurricanes when the wind speed exceeds 120 kilometers per hour (75 miles per hour). The strongest hurricane winds can reach over 290 kilometers per hour (180 miles per hour). In Asia and the western Pacific, hurricanes are referred to as "typhoons."

Swirling clouds that form during a hurricane.

When a hurricane hits land, damage is caused by both winds and flooding. The high winds can snap trees and send debris flying through the air. Some hurricane clouds even create their own tornadoes, which can cause a lot of damage in a small area.

Hurricanes cause flooding in two ways—from rain and from storm surge. First, these tropical storms carry lots of water from warm, humid regions. This water falls as heavy rain which quickly fills rivers and streams.

Next, a hurricane's strong winds also push along the ocean water in front of the storm, just like you can make a small wave if you move your hand over the surface of a puddle or pond. The water that is pushed ahead of a hurricane is called a **storm surge**. Along coastal beaches and inlets, tons of water can flood low-lying areas. Sometimes surge pushes water in streams and rivers upstream, making it even harder for rainwater to drain off the land. Damage from storm surge usually has a more lasting impact on the landscape than damage from winds.

Tornadoes

The violent wind of a tornado can cause damage to everything in its path.

Tornadoes are spiraling columns of air created by some thunderstorms. These violent wind storms cause terrible destruction when they touch down and travel along the ground. Wind speeds in the most severe tornadoes reach over 400 kilometers per hour (250 miles per hour). Around 1,000 tornadoes are reported in the United States each year. Tornadoes may cut a path of damage over 80 kilometers (50 miles) long.

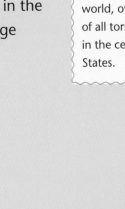

Changing Earth Fact

Though tornadoes occur in all parts of the world, over 75 percent of all tornadoes occur in the central United States.

Tornadoes often come with lightning and thunder.

Dust Storms

Sometimes a local thunderstorm will pick up dust or sediment and blow it around the sky. These kinds of dust "events" are common in areas where there are few plants to hold the soil in place. But when blowing dust covers a large area, the event is termed a dust storm. Dust storms can last from three or four hours to two or three days, and often occur in the late winter to early spring when extreme weather causes high winds.

In many areas of the Great Plains and western United States, blowing dust and sand can be common hazards. The National Weather Service issues two kinds of warnings:

- A blowing dust (blowing sand) **advisory**—issued when the presence of local windblown dust/sand reduces visibility to 400 meters (about ¼ mile) or less.

- A blowing dust (blowing sand) **warning**—issued when visibility is nearly zero.

There are many reasons to be concerned when a dust storm hits. The dust from these storms can cause breathing problems in animals and humans. Dust storms also make it hard to see. One of the most dangerous situations a person can be in is driving in a dust storm.

Global Dust Storms

When the blowing winds are strong and persistent, dust from large deserts or bare agricultural land can climb high into the atmosphere and hitch a ride to distant lands. These dust storms don't cause extensive damage and in fact they may help provide nutrients to plants on the ground where the dust settles.

Dust Storms on Mars

Earth is not the only planet in the solar system to experience dust storms. Mars is well known for its immense dust storms that often obscure the surface from our view. Recent NASA probes to Mars have shown dramatic pictures of dust storms that completely cover the surface of the planet.

12

Weathering Breaks Down Rock

Types of Weathering

There are many ways that rock breaks down. The three main types of weathering are physical, chemical, and biological weathering.

- Physical weathering is the **mechanical** breakdown of rocks and minerals.

- Chemical weathering is the **chemical** breakdown of rocks.

- **Biological weathering** is the breakdown of rock by humans, animals, and plants.

Word Connections

The term **mechanical** relates to machines or tools. For example, a jackhammer can crush and break up concrete. Similarly, a hard rock can crush a softer rock by grinding against it.

The word **chemical** relates to the way materials change when they are mixed together. For example, when salt is added to water, the salt dissolves in the water and can no longer be seen.

The term **biological weathering** relates to the physical or chemical processes involved when living things weather rock. For example, when animals such as moles and gophers dig tunnels in the earth, they contribute to rock break down.

Physical Weathering

Three of the most important types of physical weathering are abrasion, ice wedging, and exfoliation. As you already learned, abrasion is the grinding together of one rock against another.

Ice wedging happens because water often gets trapped within rocks or in the cracks of rocks. If temperatures reach below freezing at night and above freezing by day, this water repeatedly freezes and melts. Water expands when it freezes and contracts when it melts. The expansion of ice and contraction of liquid water can cause rocks to break down over time.

Ice wedging can cause rocks to break apart into small pieces.

As weathering and erosion strip away the surface of the earth, there is less weight on the buried rocks. Like a sponge that shrinks when you squeeze it and expands when you let go, the rock also expands. As it expands, cracks form along its surface. When these cracks get large enough, large slabs of rock can break off and slide away. This is called **exfoliation**.

Chemical Weathering

Rocks such as limestone and marble can easily be dissolved by water that is acidic. That's why caves and caverns form in areas with water and limestone. It's also why marble tombstones and carvings are very susceptible to damage due to chemical weathering from acid rain. The term for this type of chemical weathering is known as **dissolution**.

Scientists examine a cavern formed by the chemical weathering of rock.

Oxidation occurs when the iron in minerals meets with the oxygen in the air. The new minerals that form are weaker than the original ones and tend to break down easier. The oxidation process commonly forms rust.

Biological Weathering

The roots of plants may grow into the cracks in rocks. As the plants grow and the roots get larger, the cracks may get wider until the rock breaks. This phenomenon can occur with large plants such as trees, or small plants such as grasses.

As this tree grows, its roots may break the rock around them.

Animals, such as marmots and badgers that burrow and move through cracks in rock, can cause biological weathering that eventually shapes the landscape. Smaller creatures like beetles and ants also contribute to weathering as they channel through the earth.

Humans can contribute to biological weathering in a number of ways. We break down rock when building roads and tunnels. We also contribute to the changing landscape when we build dams and divert rivers.

Human machinery can shape the landscape in a very short time.

Weathering Processes Work Together

Physical, chemical, and biological weathering work together to break down rocks. For example, as physical weathering breaks rocks into smaller pieces, there is more surface area for chemical weathering to act on. Working together, physical, biological, and chemical weathering can more quickly break down rock.

Humans Use Rock

Stone tools were among the first inventions made by early humans. Over the centuries, humans improved their ability to shape rock for different uses. People built stone walls to mark boundaries, and they used rock to create homes. Artists learned to carve rock into beautiful statues. How many different ways do you see rocks used in the objects displayed in these photographs?

Weathering Creates Sediment and Soil

Soil is made from many kinds of sediment.

Weathering creates sediment as it breaks down rock material.
Some of this sediment becomes part of soil. Soil is a mixture of
both living and non-living things. It must provide nutrients,
water, and air to plants as well as help to physically support
them. About 45 percent of soil is weathered rock particles such
as sand, silt, or clay. The rest is composed of water (about
25 percent), air (about 25 percent), and living and decaying
plants and organisms (about 5 percent).

Earthworms live in soil.

Scientists who study soil describe soil types depending on how much sand, silt, or clay is present. This is called the **texture** of the soil. It is possible to change the texture of the soil by adding different things to it. Changing the soil means you can create the right conditions for specific plants to grow. Sandy soil has sharp edges so it feels rough when you rub it. Silty soil feels smooth and powdery when it's dry, and smooth and not sticky when it's wet. Clay is smooth when dry and sticky when wet.

Soil Provides Home to Plants and Animals

Soil is home to many plants and animals. The texture of soil affects how well plants will grow in it. For example, a soil with too much sand in it can't store enough water for most plants to grow. When the water reaches the soil, it easily drains through the relatively large spaces within the soil. Soils with a lot of clay in them, on the other hand, hold too much water. The best types of soils have a good mixture of sand, silt, and clay.

Five Important Factors in Soil Formation

- Parent material—This has to do with the type of rock and other materials that the soil is formed from. Soil parent material could be **bedrock**, it could be deposition from water, wind, or glaciers, or it could be organic material.

- Climate—The climate of a region affects how fast or slow soil formation happens. Rain, snow, wind, and other weathering forces break down the parent material.

- Life—This includes all plants and animals (including humans) living in or on the soil. The amount of water and nutrients plants need affects the way soil forms. Animals living in the soil affect what happens with waste materials and the way that soil materials will be moved around within the soil. The dead remains of plants and animals become organic matter, which enriches the soil.

- Location—The location of soil on a landscape can affect how weather can impact it. For example, soils at the bottom of a hill will get more water than soils on the slopes and soils that face the sun will be drier than soils that do not.

- Time—All of the above factors happen over time, often hundreds or thousands of years.

13

Earth Inside and Out

The Earth's Layers

The earth's surface is an amazing place, but have you ever wondered what is beneath the ground you walk on?

- Is it solid all the way through?

- Does it get colder or hotter deep inside the earth?

- What is lava and where does it come from?

Perhaps you've asked yourself one or more of these questions.

Much of what you see around you is affected by what occurs deep beneath your feet. It is hard to imagine that we are standing on a planet that is made of layers, both solid and liquid, that reach temperatures beyond anything on the earth's surface. After all, the deepest mines that humans have gone into are only about 3 kilometers (1.9 miles) beneath the surface. At those depths the rock still looks the same as that on the surface.

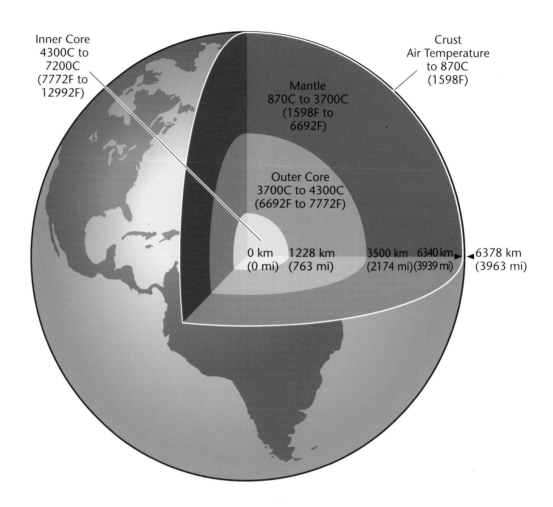

Inner Core
4300C to
7200C
(7772F to
12992F)

Crust
Air Temperature
to 870C
(1598F)

Mantle
870C to 3700C
(1598F to
6692F)

Outer Core
3700C to 4300C
(6692F to 7772F)

0 km   1228 km   3500 km   6340 km   6378 km
(0 mi)   (763 mi)   (2174 mi)(3939 mi) (3963 mi)

Word Connection

molten—Something that changes into a liquid when it is heated. **Magma** is molten rock.

The earth is made up of the following four layers:

- **Inner core**—A solid layer of iron and nickel.

- **Outer core**—A liquid layer of iron and nickel.

- **Mantle**—The thickest layer of the earth. Its upper portion is solid while its lower portion is **semi-molten** (able to flow slowly).

- **Crust**—A layer of solid rock that makes up the surface of the earth. It includes the continents and ocean basins. Compared to the other layers of the earth, the crust is a thin shell, like an egg shell.

Layer	Thickness		Temperature	
	Kilometers	**Miles**	**Celsius degrees**	**Fahrenheit degrees**
Inner Core	1228	763	4300–7200	7772–12992
Outer Core	2272	1411	3700–4300	6692–7772
Mantle	2840	1765	870–3700	1598–6692
Crust	38	24	Air temp–870	Air temp–1598

People Doing Science

How Do Scientists Know the Internal Structure of the Earth?

Scientists have used powerful drills to bore holes up to 32 kilometers (20 miles) into the earth's crust. But, even at those depths, the rock samples are similar to those found on the surface. So how did scientists figure out the internal structure of the earth?

The study of the movements produced by earthquakes is known as **seismology**. Seismology has provided many clues about how the inside of the earth looks. Two types of movements, called seismic waves, are produced during an earthquake. One type of wave can travel through solids, liquids, and gases. The second type of wave can only travel through solids. By measuring the second type of seismic wave, scientists have been able to determine that different parts of the earth are made up of solid and liquid layers.

There is still much to learn about the layers of the earth, but scientists discover more each year, as they develop new technologies and share new ideas.

Earth's Crust Moves

The earth's crust is made up of numerous pieces called **tectonic plates**. The plates float on top of a layer of hot, semi-molten rock that composes part of the mantle. The plates that float on the earth's mantle constantly move. But they move very slowly. Millions of years ago, these plates were in different places than they are today. The term "**continental drift**" is used for the idea that tectonic plates moved around in the distant past and are still moving today.

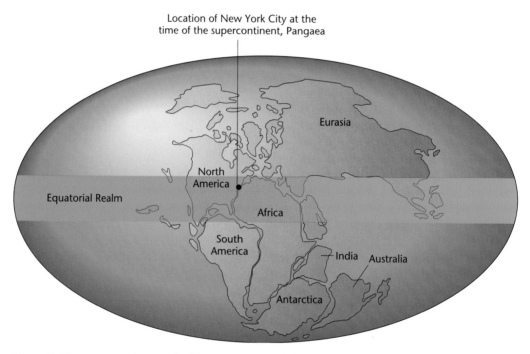

Figure 1: The supercontinent called Pangaea as it was thought to look 250 million years ago.

About 250 million years ago the earth's plates were all joined together into one landmass or supercontinent called **Pangaea** (pan-jee-uh). During that time, the continent of North America was in a different location than it is today. New York City, for example, (see Figure 1) was close to Africa.

Around 200 million years ago, Pangaea began to break apart. Figure 2 shows the current location of the earth's plates. The Earth is divided into six large plates and several other smaller ones. You can also see that some of the plates have names that are similar to the names of continents or oceans but that other plate names are unusual.

 **Think About It!**

Can you feel the earth's crust moving beneath your feet right now? What does this tell you about how fast the plates move? The earth's plates move too slowly to notice—only 1–10 cm (0.4–4 in) per year. The speed the plates move is about the same rate at which your fingernails grow.

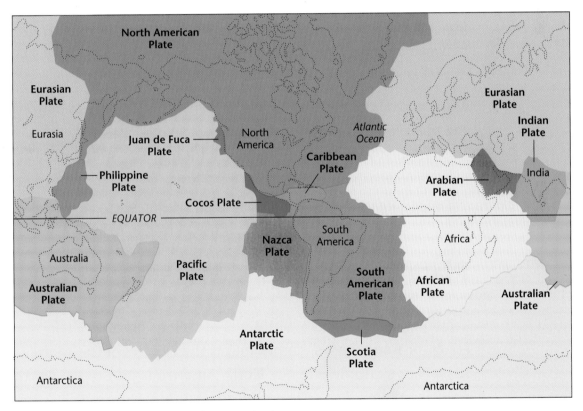

Figure 2: Current location of the earth's tectonic plates.

People Doing Science

Alfred Wegener and His Theory of Continental Drift

Alfred Wegener (1880–1930) was the first person to propose the theory of continental drift. In 1915 he wrote a book called *The Origin of Continents and Oceans*. In it he proposed the theory that there had once been a giant supercontinent, which he named Pangaea (from the Greek for "all the Earth"). He collected evidence from the various fields of earth science including geology, oceanography, and paleontology. This was one of the first times that work from different scientific areas was brought together to support a scientific theory. His evidence included the jigsaw puzzle fit between the coastlines of South America and Africa (see Figure 1) as well as similar fossil findings on both continents.

Many geologists made fun of Wegener for his ideas. It was only in the late 1960s, after more evidence of plate movement was discovered, that Wegener received credit for thinking up the theory of plate tectonics. Today, this theory is considered one of the most important theories about the earth.

Plate Boundaries

Tectonic plates contain continents as well as oceans. Their edges, or **boundaries**, do not follow the borders of the continents. For example, most of North America is part of the North American Plate. But so is part of the Atlantic Ocean.

Can you locate the boundary of the North American Plate on Figure 2? If you look closely, you should see that the eastern boundary of the North American Plate (where it meets the Eurasian Plate and African Plate) is in the middle of the Atlantic Ocean.

Many geologic events can occur where two plates meet, including earthquakes, mountain formation, and volcano formation. For example, as the Indian Plate collides with the Eurasian Plate, the Himalayan Mountains continue to rise higher each year.

In general, there are three types of plate boundaries: convergent, divergent, and transform. These terms describe what happens between two tectonic plates.

- **Convergent boundaries** occur when two plates **collide** with one another.

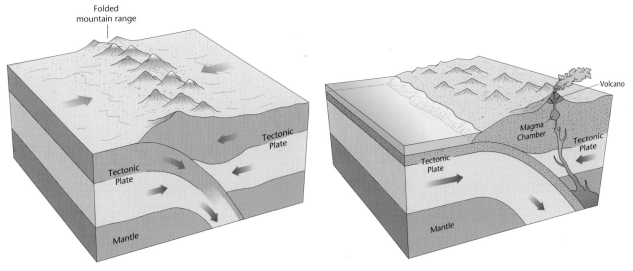

Two examples of tectonic plate collisions, resulting in mountains and volcanoes.

The Alps formed along a convergent boundary.

- **Divergent boundaries** are found where tectonic plates **move away** from each other, such as along a mid-ocean ridge. A **mid-ocean ridge** is an underwater volcanic mountain chain formed as two plates move away from each other.

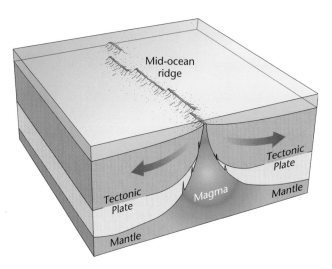

Lava erupts along the mid-ocean ridges due to underwater volcanoes. This is where the crust is weakened and stretched as the plates move apart.

As the North American Plate and Eurasian Plate move away from each other in the middle of the Atlantic Ocean, a mid-ocean ridge is forming. This ridge runs right through the country of Iceland, which is known for its active volcanoes.

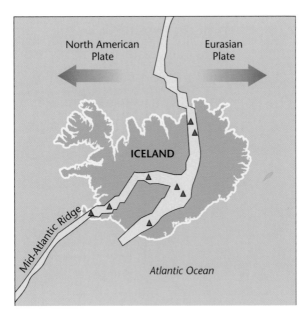

Location of Mid-Atlantic Ridge through Iceland. Note that the red triangles represent active volcanoes on the island of Iceland.

- **Transform boundaries** form when two plates **slide past** one another.

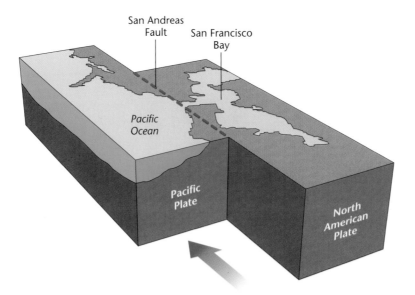

A transform boundary occurs where two plates are sliding past each other, such as in California where the Pacific Plate is sliding past the North American Plate (also known as the San Andreas fault zone).

This happens on the west coast of the United States as the Pacific Plate slides past the North American Plate. This area is known as the San Andreas fault zone. It is about 1,300 km (800 mi) long and extends through two thirds of the length of California. The Pacific Plate has been sliding northward past the North American Plate for 10 million years, at an average rate of about 5 cm (1.5 in) a year. At this rate of movement, San Francisco and Los Angeles will be side by side in about 10 million years!

San Andreas Fault, California.

Cataclysmic Events

Earthquakes, Tsunamis, and Landslides

Earthquakes cause trembling, shaking, and sometimes violent upheavals of the upper layer of earth's crust. They are caused by shifting rocks deep within the earth, or by underground movement unleashed by volcanic forces.

Widespread effects of the Loma Prieta, California, Earthquake on October 17, 1989.

Usually earthquakes produce only slight movement, but occasionally they are powerful enough to cause the surface of the earth to shake, roll, and heave. Huge cracks can open up in the ground, and buildings, bridges, and other structures may crumble.

Most of the world's earthquakes occur at fairly shallow depths, only 20 to 30 km (12–19 miles) deep. But earthquake movement often results in cataclysmic changes to the earth's surface.

Earthquakes can also trigger landslides and tsunamis. A **tsunami** is a massive wave of ocean water triggered by an earthquake or volcanic eruption on the ocean floor. Tsunamis often cause more damage than the earthquake itself and can affect coastal areas hundreds or thousands of miles away.

Tsunami damage along the waterfront at Kodiak, Alaska, 1964.

Tsunamis can travel enormous distances across the ocean and grow taller as they approach land. Where they reach shore they may attain a height of nearly 30 meters (100 feet) and can sweep very far inland.

Aerial photographs of the town of Lhoknga, Indonesia taken before and after the tsunamis of December 26, 2004.

A **landslide** is a term that includes lots of kinds of ground movement. Each of the events in this list is a landslide:

- A rock breaks from an outcrop and tumbles down a cliff

- Heavy rains soak the ground and cause mud to flow down a hillside

- An earthquake shakes the ground, causing the soil to shift and move down a slope

A landslide consisting of 600,000 tons of mud and silt slid 600 feet down a cliff face and buried nine homes in La Conchita, California, on March 4, 1995.

A landslide near McClure Pass, Colorado, in 1994.

Landslide from the Loma Prieta, California, Earthquake on October 17, 1989.

Any area that is made up of lots of loose debris resting on a slope will likely experience landslides—it's just a matter of time.

14

Mountains Build Up and Break Down

When you look at a mountain, it is hard to imagine that it did not always exist. How could something so large and majestic form? Do mountains ever change?

How Mountains Form

When the earth's tectonic plates move they can do one of three things: collide, move away from each other, or slide past one another. These plate movements can create different landforms, including mountains.

If the plates collide, several types of mountains can form. Portions of the land above the plates may be **uplifted**, or thrust upwards, creating folded mountains.

As their name implies, **folded mountains** form when two plates collide. This collision causes the crust to compress and crumple. This is similar to what happens to the hoods of cars in a head-on collision. The folds in the hood resemble mountains and valleys. The European Alps, Appalachian Mountains, and Himalayas are all examples of folded **mountain chains**.

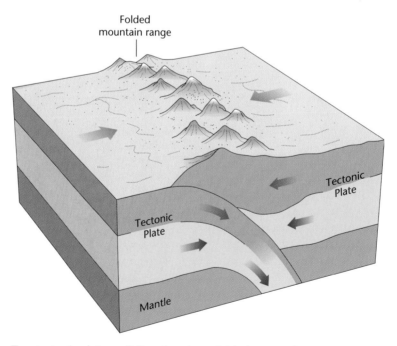

Two tectonic plates colliding, forming a folded mountain range.

The Swiss Alps.

How Mountains Break Down

Mountains are made of seemingly unbreakable rock. But like all rock, the forces of moving water, ice, and wind break them down over time. As soon as mountains form, they begin to wear down. The Appalachian Mountains, for example, were much taller and more rugged 300 million years ago, and the Himalayas may be much shorter and more rounded 300 million years from now.

Moving water from rainfall and snowmelt weathers and erodes mountain rock. So does glacial ice. Rivers carry this sediment downstream to lakes and oceans. The sediment is eventually deposited along riverbanks, floodplains, and deltas. It even flows into the ocean and settles on the ocean floor, where it may eventually become new rock.

Eventually, over millions of years, the mountains around us today will no longer exist. But thanks to deep forces beneath the earth, mountain building continues to occur, and new mountains are created.

Comparing Old and Young Mountain Ranges

🔆 Think About It!

Examine the pictures of the Appalachians and Himalayas below. Then look where the Appalachians and Himalayas are located on Figure 3. Based on what you learned about how mountains form and break down, what clues do Figure 3 and the pictures give you about which mountain range is still growing?

A section of the Appalachian Mountains in the Great Smoky Mountains National Park, Tennessee and North Carolina.

A section of the Himalayas, with Mt. Everest masked in clouds.

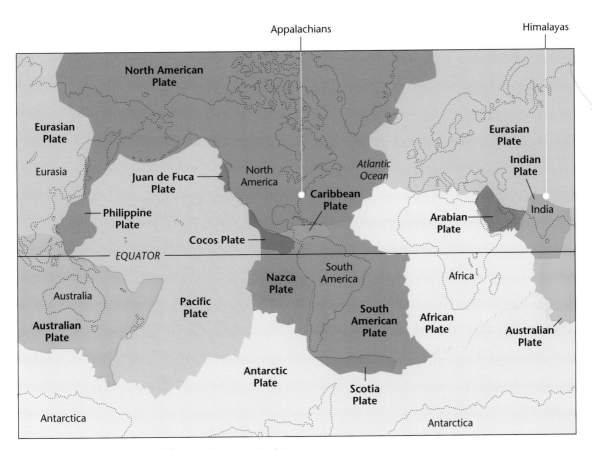

Figure 3: Current location of the earth's tectonic plates.

The Himalayas are on the boundary of two tectonic plates. If you look closely at Figure 3, you will notice that the Himalayas are located where the Indian and Eurasian Plates meet. As you learned earlier, mountain ranges form along plate boundaries.

The Himalayas are a relatively young mountain range. They began forming 60 to 45 million years ago when the Indian Plate first collided with the Eurasian Plate. They form the highest mountain range on land in the world. Mt. Everest, the tallest mountain on any continent, is 8,848 km (29,029 ft) tall! And the Himalayas are still growing! As the Indian Plate continues to collide with the Eurasian Plate, the Himalayas continue to push upward 5–10 cm (2–4 in) per year.

The Appalachians are not on the boundary of two plates. If you look closely at Figure 3, you should see that the Appalachians are located on the right side of the North American Plate. How can a mountain range be located within a plate boundary? A look into Earth's past explains this.

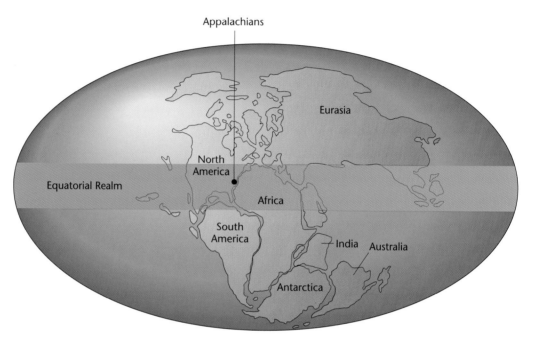

Appalachians formed as the plates that later became North America and Africa collided during the formation of Pangaea, approximately 350 million years ago.

Think About It!

Some people think that tall mountains are older because they get taller by the building up of rocks and sediment on top of the mountains. What do you think?

The story of the Appalachians began when the supercontinent Pangaea formed approximately 350 million years ago. During that time, the North American and African plates collided. The collision pushed up the earth's crust to form the Appalachian mountain chain. At that time the Appalachians were much taller than they are today.

When Pangaea began to break up about 200 million years ago, the plates began moving toward their current locations (see Figure 3). That many millions of years of weathering and erosion have reduced the Appalachians to about half their original height and much more gentle appearance than the Himalayas.

15

The Wonder of Volcanoes

There are not many events on Earth more magnificent, or dangerous, than an erupting volcano. Volcanoes are visible proof that there are forces deep within Earth that we have no control over. When and where they erupt is completely out of human hands.

Hawaii Volcanoes National Park. 1972–1974 eruption of Kilauea Volcano.

How Does a Volcano Form?

A volcano forms when **magma** (melted rock) rises through the surface of the earth. As magma deposits and builds up the earth's surface, a volcanic mountain may result. Layers of **ash** and **lava** that erupt out of the volcano also add material to the mountain.

Volcanoes channel molten rock up from a **magma chamber** deep inside the earth to an opening, or **vent,** in the center of the volcano's **summit**. The chamber and vent act like a plumbing system that pipes magma from deep inside the volcano up to the surface.

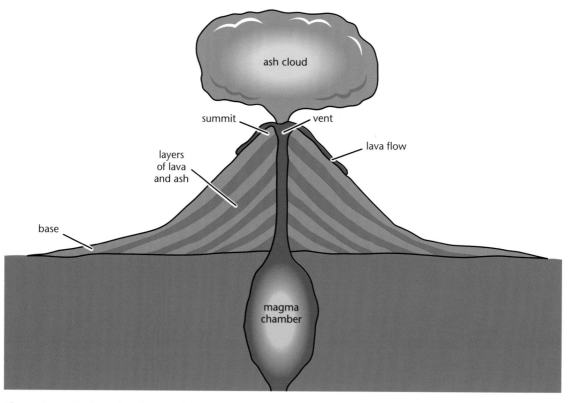

The main parts of a volcanic mountain.

Where Are Volcanoes Found?

Volcanoes are found all over the world, both on land and under the ocean. Most volcanoes are found along convergent plate boundaries or other regions known as hot spots. Some volcanoes are also found under the ocean along divergent plate boundaries, such as along a mid-ocean ridge.

Convergent Boundaries

When two tectonic plates collide to form a volcano, one plate is pushed down below the other plate. This is known as **subduction**. As the plate is pushed downward, it is melted by the heat from the layer of the earth called the mantle. Melting often causes the magma to rise to the surface. Once it reaches the surface, it may erupt quietly or explosively, forming a volcano.

Think About It!

Folded mountains form when the collision of two plates causes Earth's crust to compress and crumple. How do you think volcanic mountains form?

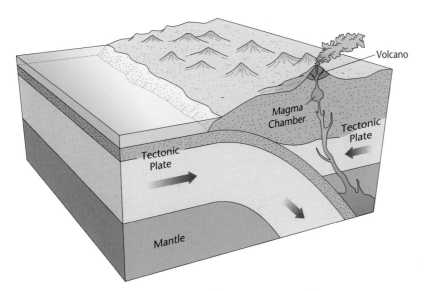

Two tectonic plates colliding, forming a volcanic mountain.

Hot Spots

A **hot spot** is a specific point on the earth's surface where magma repeatedly pushes up from the mantle and breaks through the crust. The Pacific Plate moves over the top of a giant hot spot. Magma continuously erupts from this hot spot, building the chain of volcanic mountains we know as the Hawaiian Islands.

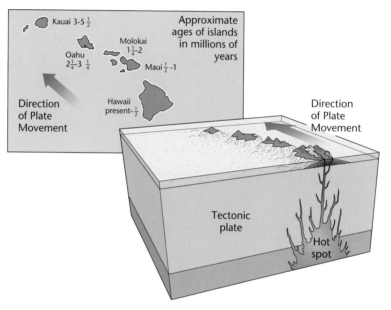

How a hot spot in the Pacific Plate formed the Hawaiian Islands.

The Ring of Fire

Although volcanoes are found on land and in seas all over the world, most volcanoes are concentrated in an area known as the "Ring of Fire." The Ring of Fire is an arc stretching from New Zealand, along the eastern edge of Asia, north across the

Aleutian Islands of Alaska, and south along the coast of North and South America. 75 percent of the world's active and dormant volcanoes on land are found along the Ring of Fire.

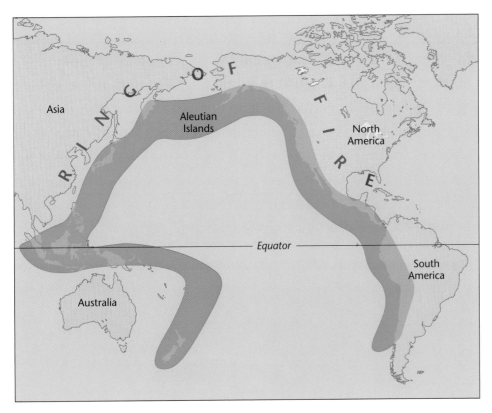

The Ring of Fire.

What makes this area such an active location for volcanoes? The Ring of Fire lies along the borders of the Pacific Plate and other plates in the area. Around the Ring of Fire, the Pacific Plate is colliding with and sliding underneath other plates. As these plates move, they change the earth's surface along their boundaries, creating volcanic eruptions and earthquakes.

Volcano Legends

The Klamath Indians of the Pacific Northwest tell a legend about a fight between two chiefs. Llao was the chief of the Below World and was at Mount Mazama in Oregon. Skell was the chief of the Above World and stood at the summit of Mount Shasta in northern California. The two mountains are only a hundred miles apart. As darkness covered the land the two chiefs threw rocks and flames at each other. Llao, injured, fell back inside of Mount Mazama and was never seen again. A huge hole was left where he fell into the Below World. Over time, the hole filled with water to make Crater Lake—a **caldera** that formed by large volcanic eruption and collapse of a volcanic cone about 6,800 years ago.

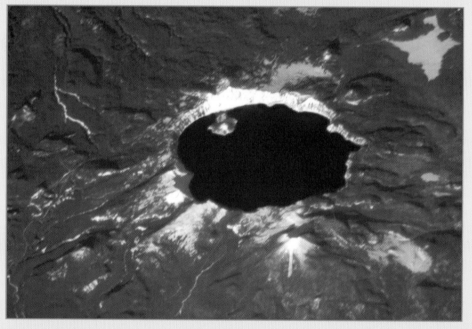

Crater Lake, Oregon.

Types of Volcanic Eruptions

Eruptions can vary from highly explosive ones that eject rocks, ash, and lava to quiet ones with flowing streams of lava.

Magma with a large amount of volcanic gases results in enormous, explosive eruptions. As the magma rises, the volcanic gases separate from the magma to form bubbles. This increases the pressure under the volcano. When the pressure becomes too great, the volcano erupts. These eruptions often send up a massive **ash cloud** high into the atmosphere.

Magma with a small amount of volcanic gases results in quiet eruptions. This is because the pressure under the volcano is not as great. In quiet eruptions, fluid lava flows from the summit of the volcano rather than sending an ash cloud into the atmosphere.

 **Think About It!**

Have you ever put your thumb over an opened bottle of soda, shook it vigorously, and then quickly removed your thumb? What happened? Did the soda explode out of the bottle? A similar thing happens when a volcano erupts.

Word Connection

Volcanic activity—Any volcano that has erupted within the past two hundred years and that still shows signs of possibly erupting again is considered to be **active**. Volcanoes that have not erupted in the past two hundred years, but are considered likely to erupt again, are called **dormant**. Volcanoes unlikely to ever erupt again are considered to be **extinct**.

Types of Volcanic Mountains

There are three main types of volcanic mountains that each shape the earth's surface in very different ways: composite volcanoes, shield volcanoes, and cinder cones.

Composite Volcanoes

Composite volcanoes are steep, cone-shaped volcanoes. They form from highly explosive, repeated eruptions over time. They are located at convergent boundaries where two plates collide. Mt. St. Helens and Mt. Rainier in Washington State, Mt. Vesuvius and Mt. Etna in Italy, and Mt. Fuji in Japan are examples of composite volcanoes.

Mt. St. Helens prior to eruption. Washington State, May 17, 1980.

Mt. St. Helens during eruption. Washington State, May 18, 1980.

Mt. St. Helens after eruption. Washington State, September 8, 1980.

Shield Volcanoes

Shield volcanoes are broad, rounded volcanic mountains with a characteristic "shield," or flat dome shape. They form from less explosive, ongoing eruptions that occur for many years. Eruptions from shield volcanoes usually come out of a central vent.

Over time, thousands of repeated **lava flows** build shield volcanoes. Shield volcanoes are often located over hot spots. The Hawaiian Islands are examples of shield volcanoes that have formed over a hot spot in the Pacific Plate.

Scientists also believe that a hot spot exists in the region of Yellowstone National Park in northwestern Wyoming. Although not actively erupting, the magma under the surface fuels more than 10,000 hot springs, **geysers** (like Old Faithful), and bubbling **mudpots** (pools of boiling mud).

Mauna Ulu eruption of Kilauea Volcano. Fountains of lava flowing from vents on the east side of Mauna Ulu. Hawaiian Volcanoes National Park.1969–1971.

> ### Changing Earth Fact
>
> The biggest volcano in the world is Mauna Loa, in Hawaii. This shield volcano rises 29,000 feet from the floor of the ocean.

Old Faithful geyser erupting in Yellowstone National Park.

Cinder Cones

Cinder cones are small volcanoes shaped like cones. They have a bowl-shaped crater at the summit and rarely rise more than 300 meters (1000 feet) or so above their surroundings. They form from broken pieces of ejected lava and cinders. **Cinders** are small pieces of solid volcanic rock.

Cinder cone eruptions are generally much smaller and less explosive than most composite volcanoes. They are often found on shield volcanoes and occur because their magma has more gas than the surrounding shield volcano eruptions. This makes their eruptions more explosive. There are lots of cinder cones in western North America.

Lassen Volcanic National Park, California. Lava flows at the base of the Cinder Cone. One flow is covered with thick cinders (yellowish brown area); the other flow is black (no cinders). 1977.

Cataclysmic Events

Volcanoes Cause Other Cataclysmic Events

Explosive Volcanic Eruptions

Explosive volcanic eruptions are among the most dangerous and stunning cataclysmic events on the earth. A violent eruption can completely transform the landscape for hundreds of miles around a volcano.

The force and heat from the eruption can cause **pyroclastic flows**—avalanches of hot gases, ash, rock, and lava that flow downhill under the influence of gravity. These pyroclastic flows can destroy virtually everything in the vicinity of the volcano.

Lahars

Explosive eruptions may also cause **lahars**, a mudslide that flows down the sides of a volcanic mountain.

A lahar caused by the 1980 eruption of Mt. St. Helens.

A building covered by the mudflow.

This is what happened in Washington State in 1980 when ice and snow on the peak of Mt. St. Helens melted during an explosive eruption. The sudden surge of water down the river valleys carried enormous floods of ash and mud. People living in the shadow of other volcanoes in the Pacific Northwest have warning systems to alert them if there is danger from a lahar.

A lahar can also be triggered by an earthquake or heavy rains, or by a combination of these events. For example, earthquakes and heavy tropical rainstorms can affect the volcanoes of Central America. A particularly heavy rainfall on the slopes of a volcanic mountain can release a torrent of muddy ash. Or, an earthquake can cause volcanic ash and rock to fall into a river, creating a lahar.

Whatever the cause, lahars can be more devastating than an actual eruption, burying buildings, farmland, animals, and people beneath tons of volcanic ash and sediment.

An aerial view of Mt. Ruahpehu, a volcanic mountain in New Zealand. Can you see how the farmland in the lower left might be threatened by a volcanic eruption or lahar?

A Tour of Desert Landforms

Picture yourself as an explorer seeing the landscape in the photograph below for the first time. Imagine how you'd feel if you never knew it existed.

In 1876, T.C Bailey, a land surveyor, had these words to say about the Bryce Canyon landscape:

"The surface breaks off ...to a depth of several hundred feet...There are thousands of red, white, purple, and vermillion colored rocks of all sizes... There are deep caverns and rooms resembling ruins of prisons, castles, churches, with their guarded walls, battlements, spires and steeples... [It is] the wildest and the most wonderful scene that the eye of man ever beheld, in fact, it is one of the wonders of the world."

Read on for a quick guided tour of a few fascinating landforms.

Canyons

Bryce Canyon, as well as many other deep canyons, began to take shape millions of years ago. The rock in this canyon was originally deposited as sediment at the bottom a large inland sea. Over time, the sediment converted to rock. Then the sea disappeared and the rock was left open to the weather. Ancient rivers carved deep gullies in the rock and helped to sculpt pillars and towers.

It probably took millions of years for this canyon to be created.

During rainfall, streams of water flow over the rock and can weather and erode the landscape. Rainfall can also enter the cracks in the pillars, towers, and other formations. If the water in the cracks repeatedly freezes and thaws, the rocks can break down and fall apart due to these forces.

Rainfall is also responsible for much of the weathering and erosion that creates desert landforms. When the infrequent rain does come to a desert, it is sometimes very heavy. Since some ground in the desert is hard and compact, the rainwater may not soak in. This large amount of water creates a number of short-lived streams which weave their way through the desert landscape and carve up the earth.

Arches

Rainfall can act in several ways to shape these rare natural bridges. Sometimes water dissolves the grains that cement the rock together. Cracks then form in the rock. This provides a way for water to flow into cracks. The rocks are then subject to physical weathering such as the freezing and thawing of water.

A rock arch is often formed because the rock around the outside of the arch is often harder to break down than the rock in the middle of the arch.

Arches like this are very rare.

Badlands

Badlands are found where the rocks and sediment of a landscape are fairly loose and weak. This makes them easily weathered and eroded by water. Badlands generally have steep slopes and an intricate web of stream beds. The stream beds are usually dry except for periods of heavy rainfall.

Fossil hunters like to search in badlands because a lot of rock is often exposed to the air for the first time after a heavy rainfall.

Badlands are notoriously easy to get lost in since each of the many stream beds looks very similar.

Badlands in South Dakota.

Mesas and Buttes

Mesas and buttes can be seen for miles in the **Four Corners** region of the United States.

Mesas are tall, massive, isolated rock formations with flat tops. The flat tops make them look something like tables for desert-dwelling giants. Mesas can be hundreds of feet high and often have sides that are very steep and often nearly vertical. The rock that forms mesas is often very resistant to any type of weathering or erosion. When a mesa forms, the softer rock around it weathers and erodes away. The hard rock that forms the mesa is then left behind to decorate the landscape.

Word Connection

Mesa is the Spanish word for table.

A large mesa in the background.

Buttes are generally considered to be smaller versions of mesas. If a rock formation has many features of a mesa, but is too small to resemble a table, then geologists call it a butte.

This butte is made out of sandstone.

Glossary

active volcano

A volcano that is currently erupting or has recently erupted (within the past 300 years) and that is likely to erupt again in the near future.

abrasion

The grinding down of one rock by another.

advance

To move forward.

alpine lake

A lake that forms high up in the mountains as a result of glacial meltwater or snow melt filling a cirque or natural depression.

ash

Tiny particles of broken-down rock blown into the air when a volcano erupts.

ash cloud

A very large amount of ash ejected high into the air during a volcanic eruption.

ash fall

Volcanic ash that deposits on the ground.

atmosphere

The thin layer of gases—mostly nitrogen (78%), oxygen (21%), other gases and water vapor (1%)—surrounding Earth. The air all around us.

backwash

A backward flow of water.

barrier island

A long, narrow island running parallel to the shoreline, built up by the action of waves.

base

The lowest part of a mountain.

basin

An area of land drained by a river and the streams and creeks that feed that river.

bedrock

The solid unweathered layer of rock beneath the earth's surface.

biological weathering
The breakdown of rock by humans, animals, and plants.

boundary
The edge or border of something.

breakwaters
Structures built by humans to prevent erosion of a shoreline.

caldera
A large crater formed by volcanic explosion or by collapse of a volcanic cone.

canyon
A deep valley with steep sides shaped by water.

cap rock
A layer of rock that resists erosion.

cataclysmic event
An event that causes a sudden and dramatic change to the earth's surface.

chemical
The way materials change when they are mixed together.

chemical weathering
The chemical breakdown of rocks.

cinder cone
A steep conical volcano that is built up of bits of lava and cinders. Cinder cones are generally much smaller and less explosive than composite volcanoes.

cinders
Small pieces of solid volcanic rock.

cirque
A deep bowl-shaped depression that a glacier carved out of a mountainside. Cirques usually have steep sides.

climate
The average weather for a particular place over time.

compact fluorescent bulb (CFL)
A type of light bulb that contains a gas in the tube and a special material on the glass of the tube. When electricity transfers through it, energy transfers to the gas and then to the special material, which gives off the energy as light.

composite volcano
A volcanic mountain built up by accumulations of lava and ash. This type of volcano usually has steep sides and very explosive eruptions.

compressed
Made smaller by squeezing.

conserve
To use carefully or sparingly; to avoid wasting a material.

constructive waves
A low wave that deposits material after it breaks, building up a beach.

continental drift
The idea that tectonic plates moved around in the distant past and are still moving today.

continental glacier
Sheets of glacial ice that cover a large expanse of land, such as Greenland or Antarctica.

convergent boundary
The boundary between two tectonic plates that are colliding and pushing directly into each other.

core
The center of the earth. It is composed mostly of iron. It has two parts: a molten (not solid) outside and a solid (hard) inside.

crust
The outside layer of the earth's surface. It is made of solid rock.

crystal
A solid material with a pattern that repeats over and over. Minerals form as crystals.

delta
A landform at the mouth of a river made by the sand, silt, soil, and rocks deposited by moving water.

deposition
The process in which water, wind, or ice build up the earth's surface by dropping sediment in new locations.

describe
To use words to tell about something, such as an observation.

destructive wave
A high wave with a strong backwash that erodes material after it breaks, causing the beach to deteriorate.

dissolution
The process of being dissolved. Caverns form when calcium-rich rocks, such as limestone, are dissolved by acidic rainwater.

divergent boundary
The boundary between two tectonic plates that are moving directly away from each other.

dormant volcano
A volcano that is not currently erupting, but that geologists believe may erupt again.

drought
Extremely dry weather for a long period of time, with little or no rainfall. Droughts usually cause water shortages.

earthquake
Shaking or trembling of the earth's crust due to volcanic forces or the shifting of tectonic plates deep underground.

erosion
The process in which gravity, water, ice, and wind move sediment from one place to another on the earth's surface.

erratic
A large rock moved and dropped by a glacier far from where it originated.

eruption
When a volcano ejects magma, ash, and gases onto the earth's surface or into the earth's atmosphere.

evaporate
The process of a liquid changing into an invisible gas.

exfoliation
A type of physical weathering in which buried rock expands as surface rock erodes, causing the buried rock layer to crack and break off.

extinct volcano
A volcano that is not currently erupting and that is unlikely to ever erupt again.

feature
A noticeable characteristic or trait.

flood
An overflowing of water onto land; this occurs when there is more water than a river can hold.

floodplain
A flat area of land stretching out on either side of a river.

folded mountains
Mountains that form when collisions of the earth's plates crumple and fold the earth's crust.

fossil
A rock whose shape reveals information about an ancient plant, animal, or other organism.

Four Corners
A location in the southwest United States where the boundaries of four states—Colorado, New Mexico, Arizona, and Utah—meet.

geologist
A scientist who studies geology.

geology
The science that involves the study of the earth, including its history and the processes that shape it.

geyser
A natural hot spring that periodically ejects a column of water and steam into the air.

glacial polish
The smooth, shiny appearance of rock caused by movement of a glacier.

glacial striations
Long scratches in rock caused by movement of a glacier.

glacier
A large, long-lasting mass of moving ice and snow. Glaciers move downhill or outward in all directions as a result of gravity and their immense weight; they retreat (shrink) as a result of melting.

global warming
An increase in the average temperature of the earth's atmosphere, especially a lasting increase that causes the climate to change.

gravity
The force that attracts all objects toward the center of the earth.

greenhouse effect
When gases in the earth's atmosphere trap heat energy from the sun's rays, causing an increase in average global temperatures.

greenhouse gases
A group of gases—including water vapor, carbon dioxide, methane, ozone, and other gases—that trap the sun's heat energy in Earth's atmosphere, producing a greenhouse effect.

gypsum
A colorless, white, or yellowish mineral used to make a variety of plaster products and fertilizers.

headwaters
The streams from which a river originates. Also known as *source*.

hoodoo
A strangely-shaped rock formation, sculpted by water erosion.

horn

A peak with many steep sides carved by small glaciers.

hot spot

A specific point on the earth's surface where magma repeatedly pushes up from the mantle and breaks through the crust.

hurricanes

Violent tropical cyclone storms with torrential rains and wind speeds of more than 117 kilometers (73 miles) per hour.

hydrologist

A scientist who studies water.

Ice Age

The most recent period when the earth became colder and much of the earth was covered by glacial ice.

ice wedging

A type of physical weathering where water trapped in tiny rock cracks freezes and expands, causing the rock to break.

igneous rock

Rock that forms when molten rock cools and hardens.

incandescent bulb

A type of light bulb that contains a metal filament, or wire, that becomes very hot when electricity transfers through it. This produces light.

Industrial Revolution

A period, beginning about 250 years ago, when the work done by machines in factories began to replace the work done by hand at home.

kettle

A small, scooped-out area left by the melted ice of a glacier. When filled with water, may become a pond or lake.

lahar

A mudslide that flows down the sides of a volcanic mountain.

landform

A part of the earth's surface that has a unique shape, is easy to recognize, and was created by nature.

landscape

A large area of land that includes a wide variety of surface features, such as hills, valleys, and rivers.

landslide

A mass of rocks, soil, and debris that suddenly slides down a steep slope.

lava

Magma that flows onto the earth's surface.

lava flow

A stream of magma that flows onto the earth's surface during a volcanic eruption.

levee
A mound of dirt that acts like a wall to contain water when floods occur.

magma
Melted rock inside the earth.

magma chamber
A cavity, or hollow space, deep inside the earth that contains magma.

mantle
The layer below the earth's crust. It is much thicker than other layers and its lower portion has a semi-molten, slowly flowing consistency.

meander
To curve, or follow a winding path.

mechanical
Relating to machines or tools.

mental model
A model someone is thinking about in their mind.

mesa
Tall, massive, isolated rock formations with flat tops.

metamorphic rock
Rock that forms when other rocks change because of chemical reactions, heat, pressure, or all three.

mid-ocean ridge
An underwater volcanic mountain chain formed as two plates move away from each other.

minerals
The basic ingredients of rocks. Minerals form as crystals, although sometimes the crystals are too small to see.

model
An object that represents something that is similar to the real thing in many ways (it might be made out of the same materials), but is different in some ways (it might be much bigger or smaller, for example).

molten
Something that changes into a liquid when it is heated.

moraine
Hill-like piles of unsorted rocks and sediment dropped by a glacier.

mountain
A part of the earth's crust that was raised during plate collisions. A mountain is at least 300 meters (985 feet) higher than surrounding land.

mountain chain
A group of mountains clustered together.

mouth
Where a river meets a lake, valley, or ocean.

mudpot
A pool of boiling mud.

mushroom rocks
Rock formations that are narrow on the bottom (base) and wider at the top.

native plant
A plant that is found naturally in a given local area, rather than one that is brought in from another region.

observe
To use your senses to pay close attention to something and notice many details about it.

oxidation
The process in which oxygen combines with an element or substance, such as iron. Oxidation is a major cause of chemical weathering.

Pangaea
One landmass or supercontinent of the earth's plates that existed about 250 million years ago.

physical model
A three-dimensional model of something.

physical weathering
The mechanical breakdown of rocks and minerals.

pictorial model
A two-dimensional model of something.

pyroclastic flow
An avalanche of hot ash, rock fragments, and gas that rushes down the side of a volcano during an eruption. Pyroclastic flows move fast and destroy nearly all objects in their way.

reservoir
A human-made lake behind a dam.

retreat
To move backwards.

river
A body of flowing water that empties into an ocean, valley, lake, or another river.

riverbank
The sides of a river.

riverbed
The bottom of a river.

river channel
The bed and banks of a stream or river.

rock pillar
A tall column of rock.

sand dune
A hill of loose sand formed by the wind.

seawall
A structure built by humans to prevent erosion of a shoreline.

sediment
Materials, such as sand, silt, soil, and rocks, that have been carried along and deposited by water, wind, or ice.

sedimentary rock
Rock that forms when sediment or the remains of plants and animals are cemented together.

seismology
The study of the movements produced by earthquakes.

semi-molten
Able to flow slowly.

shield volcano
A volcano with a broad, rounded shape. Shield volcanic eruptions are typically not explosive, and the lava is more fluid than in composite volcanic eruptions.

shoreline
A boundary line between land and water.

slope
The inclined surface of a hill or mountain.

soil
A mixture of rock, sediment, and organic material, including living and dead plants, insects, and bacteria.

source
Where a river begins. Also known as *headwaters*.

stabilize
To keep from moving.

storm surge
The water that is pushed ahead of a hurricane.

stream-gaging station
A building that houses instruments for measuring the water flow in a stream or river.

subduction
An area where the edge of a tectonic plate is pulled down into the mantle below another plate.

summit
The highest part of a volcanic mountain.

tectonic plate
A large piece of the earth's fractured crust.

texture
A description of soil based on how much sand, silt, or clay it contains.

tornado
A violent spiraling column of air that is generated by a thunderstorm cloud. Tornadoes have wind speeds of 160 to 480 kilometers (100 to 300 miles) per hour.

transform boundary
The boundary between two tectonic plates that are sliding past each other.

tsunami
A huge wave of ocean water that hits land and is caused by an earthquake, landslide, or volcanic eruption under the ocean.

uplift
To thrust upwards. The process of raising a portion of the earth's crust when tectonic plates collide.

valley
The low land between mountains or hills.

vent
An opening in the earth's crust where magma, ash, and volcanic gases escape.

volcanic mountain
Mountains that form when volcanic materials are deposited on earth's surface over time.

volcano
An opening in the earth's crust and the deposits that result when volcanic materials are released through it from inside the earth.

wave energy
The energy in the motion of a wave.

waves
The up and down movement of water in a lake or ocean.

weathering
The breaking down of rocks into smaller pieces.

wetland
An area of land that is covered with water, such as a bog, marsh, or swamp. The water may be there all year, or it may disappear during certain seasons.

wind
Air that is in motion over the surface of the earth.

windbreak
An object or material, such as a fence or row of trees, that blocks the path of the wind.

Credits

Illustrations

Every effort has been made to secure permission and provide appropriate credit for illustrations and in subsequent editions we will correct any errors called to our attention. Unless otherwise acknowledged, all illustrations are the property of Chicago Science Group.

12, 37, 38, 44, 48, 59, 63, 67, 90, 110, 111, 113, 114, 115, 122, 125, 126, 129, 130, 131 Lineworks, Inc.; **24** Bill Reiswig; **72, 108, 128** Colin Hayes

Photographs

Every effort has been made to secure permission and provide appropriate credit for photographic material and in subsequent editions we will correct any errors called to our attention. Unless otherwise acknowledged, all photographs are the property of Chicago Science Group.

Photo locators denoted as follows: Top (T), Center (C), Bottom (B), Left (L), Right (R), Background (Bkgd).

Cover: U.S. Fish and Wildlife Service, Photos.com, U.S. Fish and Wildlife Service, Austin Post, U.S. Geological Survey, S.W. Lohman, U.S. Geological Survey, W.B. Hamilton, U.S. Geological Survey; **Chapter 1:** 1 (B) Mark Emery, U.S. Fish and Wildlife Service; 2 (T) W.B. Hamilton, U.S. Geological Survey, (B) W.B. Hamilton, U.S. Geological Survey; 3 (T) W.B. Hamilton, U.S. Geological Survey, (B) Photos.com; 4 (T) U.S. Army Corps of Engineers, (B) U.S. Army Corps of Engineers; **Chapter 2:** 8 (B) R.L. Christiansen, U.S. Geological Survey; 9 (T) U.S. Geological Survey, (B) E.D. McKee, U.S. Geological Survey; 11 (T) ClipArt.com; 13 (T) U.S. Geological Survey; 14 (CL) ClipArt.com, (BL) ClipArt.com, (B) ClipArt.com; **Chapter 3:** 15 (B) Lance Campbell; 16 (T) Lance Campbell, (B) Photos.com; 17 (T) Lance Campbell; 18 (B) Photos.com; 19 (B) Photos.com; 20 (B) Photos.com; 21 (B) Photos.com; 22 (C) Photos.com; **Chapter 4:** 23 (CR) Photos.com; **Chapter 5:** 29 (CR) Photos.com; 31 (C) Photos.com; 32 (C) W.B. Hamilton, U.S. Geological Survey; 33 (C) Photos. com; 34 (T) NASA Johnson Space Center—Earth Sciences and Image Analysis

Index